Using the Inner Art of Dowsing in the Search for My Spiritual Enlightenment

Written and Compiled with Love
by
Anneliese Gabriel Hagemann
and
Doris Katharine Hagemann

3 H Dowsing International®

Anneliese's address:
    3 H Dowsing International
    Anneliese Gabriel Hagemann
    W10160, County Road C
    Wautoma, WI 54982 U.S.A.

Telephone contact for Anneliese in Wautoma, WI:
    Tel.   1-920-787-4747 Wautoma, WI
    FAX   1-920-787-2006

Telephone contact for Anneliese in Mesa, AZ
    Tel.   1-480-986-6720

E-mail address for Anneliese:
    ilovedowsing@hotmail.com

This book may be purchased and used for educational purposes.
For information, contact Anneliese at the postal address or a phone number listed above.
See the Bibliography for a list of other books published by 3 H Dowsing International.

First edition published 2002 by 3 H Dowsing International.
Cover designed by Doris Katharine Hagemann.
First edition edited by Katheryn J. Wicker.

ISBN: 0965665348

Library of Congress Number: 2001012345

TABLE OF CONTENTS

INDEX TO MESSAGES

INSPIRED MESSAGES

Using the Inner Art of Dowsing in the Search for My Spiritual Enlightenment

Verses from the Bible

PREFACE

Money has replaced religion as the opiate of the masses.   *Karl Marx*

Karl Marx has pieces that still ring true. We have been educated, yes, but it has become an education of consumerism. Go after almighty money and all that it can buy us. We think it makes us happy… satisfied… fulfilled…

Ha! And inside, we echo hollow… empty… Looking again for the item to solve it. Perhaps it is in drugs that money can buy; the prescriptions; the experiments on psyche, mind and body for whatever ails us.

And further lost we become, deeper into confusion… numbness… disparity…

Or perhaps the solution is in that new, fast, shiny car, so we can zoom ahead of all, in our own shiny bright package—traveling faster, quicker, sharper than anyone.

Hmmm… a giant house with a big back yard, or candy brightly colored showing the rainbow, sucking us along its colored arch. Or is it that fast bite with a jolly prize of plastic? Or is the solution whatever else we choose to lose ourselves in, the opiate of consumerism?

How sad. We are the richest nation, and yet we are blinded and numb, circling in our own world, not knowing that every choice/decision/manipulation we make affects all people, all places, all life.

When we begin to awaken, and refuse to let things put us back to sleep, we realize and remember that to be here as true beings is to keep in balance with all and realize we are so much more than money, power or riches can buy. Illusions we create for ourselves are many and powerful. There must be diligence if we are to walk through this.

We have even forgotten how to treat each other as humans, beings who all share the same heritage, all spirits residing on this planet that allows us to eventually be able to manifest any thought or idea into a reality.

What is it that we are striving for? To see that we are here only to learn and share, that we belong to something so much bigger… brighter… all encompassing… beyond us… beyond this physical perspective we hold so dear in our minds.

With that social commentary, let me introduce some tools that may be used in the search towards the Enlightenment for which we all strive.

Doris Hagemann

As I gather more information to share with others, I am so touched by the grace of God, by the ability to bring forth the Truth; to live in harmony, peace, and total Truth; to honor and respect; to live without condition; to blend with each and everyone on Earth; to be a warrior inspired by others to move on, and then come together at harvest time with treasures of healing medicine, may it be coffee, children, plants, animals, or jewelry. Each of them has its own healing power of God.

Thank you. Amen.

Anneliese Hagemann

I've been blessed twice over while editing the first edition of this work: reading the text brightens my mind; and being in contact with Anneliese, a woman with a joyful heart, lifts my spirit. To investigate and resolve my health issues, I learned from Anneliese how to dowse, one of the Divine Tools for Spiritual Enlightenment described herein. Perhaps it's time for me to learn to wield additional tools.

Katheryn Wicker

DEDICATION

I dedicate this book to the Enlightenment of every Human Being on this Earth.

Blessings of Divine Love and Light.

Anneliese Hagemann

INTRODUCTION

In the past five years, since Doris and I wrote our first book, we have found that Spiritual Enlightenment is the underlying goal of all who search for Truth—gaining awareness of who we are, our purpose in this lifetime, and connecting with the Highest Source. With this text, we hope to assist people in their search. As have all others who travel this road, we recognize there are many ways to increase one's awareness, knowledge, and wisdom. By presenting the technique of dowsing/divining, we hope to give you more direct access to tools and paths that may be considered.

We wish you Light, Love, and Truth in your search.

Anneliese and Doris Hagemann

Why Do We Yearn for Spiritual Enlightenment?

Souls were all once part of the DIVINE. Ancient sources speak of how we separated or pulled ourselves away from the Light. (Adam and Eve made conscious choices; Buddhists speak of getting caught in lower levels of consciousness or rebirth/regrowth of the Soul.) We have all separated at one time or another. Separation is to disunite, to divide, to part, to sever, to disconnect. We all have traversed to the Darkness, been separated from the Light, moved into the unawareness, the shadow. All of us have, in one way or another, moved away the furthest we could from the Source. We have entwined ourselves in this physical realm, mistaking human beliefs of reality for the Truth and thus have turned away from the TRUTH or DIVINE REALITY. By these independent choices we took ourselves away, and now by independent choices we choose to return.

With Spiritual Enlightenment, we recognize that our true business on this earthly plane is to learn, to share and to grow. You have a choice in this lifetime to complete unfinished business with your family, your work environment, relationships, etc. Look and see where you need to work, where to free yourself. To Enlighten means to let go of everything and commit yourself to the Divine Source (substitute your name—God, Buddhist Dharma, Higher Power, Universal Consciousness, Allah, Jehovah, Mother Mary, etc.—for the Vibration to which you relate).

A BEING, IN GOD'S EYES

What is a Human Being in God's eyes? A Hub, a Spoke in a Wheel, a Connection, an Instrument for presenting the Divine Principles of Truth.

What is a Normal Human Being in God's Eyes? One who has all the gifts but often forgets to use them. Their task is to bring forth and use previous knowledge.

What is a Supernatural Human Being in God's Eyes? A Supporter; one who is beyond Humanness in connection with another world; one who represents time, space, power of conducting descended principles of sounds from source or origin.

What is a Weird Human being in God's Eyes? One who has other duties to perform but is captured in a human body, and who discovers, finds out and is influenced by Supernatural practitioners beyond this world.

If we choose to live in the shadow of our Soul, we are not growing, and we return to the uncivilized time of our being, not relating to the Source. Being detached from our Soul is being detached from God.

A letter to ourselves: Staying in balance at all times, helps us stay in the Truth with the Higher Source. Then we are not allowing our Will to get in the way of God's Will.

Again: do not give up your Soul for the price of greed.

It does not matter how old we are, where we were born or what religion we practice. Nothing really matters in the way we choose to live our lives. What matters is this: we came in as a pure Soul-being, as a pure creation of God, but why did we tarnish his Image?

We need to ask ourselves, "Can we go back and embrace the Truth?" The answer is, "Yes we can." Embrace the purity of the Divine, and be Divine forever.

THE COMPANY WE KEEP

With whom do we associate or compare ourselves? Is it our mother, father, brother, sister, our neighbor, the church-being we sit next to, our work-associated being? We need to look at ourselves.

My children, the only one we need to associate with is the Divine Source, God the Truth within.

Having gone as far away as we can, we now are on our return journey.

The journey back to the SOURCE is the journey for our Spiritual Enlightenment. And the question is, "How do we find the path that we lost so long ago?"

WHAT DOES IT MEAN—THE SEARCH FOR MY SPIRITUAL EN "LIGHTEN" MENT?

Let us begin the journey by investigating the words "Search," "Spiritual," and "Enlightenment" to clarify meaning and intent. It is often highly beneficial to look at actual meanings of words to understand their original intended use, to better understand exactly what you are saying now.

The Search

As noted in the Introduction, we are all searching. We are all on a quest to find the Source, TRUTH, universal God, harmony, "the Way" (Dao or Tao), or whatever we choose to call the Higher Power.

There is not one single path. Our search leads us on paths unique to our individuality. We each have our own perspective and understanding of the Higher Power. Differences in views and approaches need not invalidate other approaches or beliefs. Possibilities of healing and understanding are as infinite as the universe. If you feel inner guidance to investigate use of crystals, or to accept fellowship and devotion offered by a church, or to study chakra energy, or to seek out other teachings and methods, then do it. Be open to alternatives that you may not have previously considered or encountered. Each person eventually develops insights to what they encounter.

To **quest** is to go in search of, inquire, to seek and pursue (moving forward). This questing need not be part of a religion, but rather can be part of an individual's spirituality.

Spiritual

"Spiritual" means pertaining to or consisting of Spirit.

"Spirit" means Breath, Life, the Immaterial, and the Immortal part of man. "Divine Spirit" is spirit relating to sacred things.

Spirituality is the expression of human beings' search for greater meaning in life beyond materialism. Materialism (a doctrine that denies existence of spirit) emphasizes satisfaction of bodily wants and achieving physical comfort and success.

Problems are opportunities disguised. We complain and use the word "hard" or "difficult" about a situation we're in. What happens, though, is that our subconscious mind accepts those words as truth (reality), and by that we burden ourselves and see only the negative part of the situation. Instead, we can choose to accept the situation as a Divine Gift of growth.

We must look *inward* in our search:
   I–Inward *N*–Needs *W*–Wholeness *A*–And *R*–Recovery of *D*–Divineness

Our need, now, is "immunity" to earthly desires.

En "Lighten" Ment

"Enlighten" is to illuminate, to furnish knowledge, to instruct, to give spiritual insight to. The act of enlightening is to enlighten; lighten; to make light; to gain insight, knowledge, and awareness; to free from ignorance or misconception; to gain a full comprehension of problems involved. According to Buddhism, Enlightenment is a final blessed state marked by the absence of desire or suffering.

"Lighten" is to make light or clear and shining; to become Light; to dissipate darkness; to make light and clean; mental and spiritual illumination, knowledge, information;

standing in God's Light; discovery; detection; be light-hearted.

&—&—&—&—&—&—&

Listening to your Inner Knowing, keeps your Divine Light glowing.

Lighthearted with the flow, is the only way to go on
our way of Enlightenment.

Let the radiating, healing Light and Love manifest in your heart and Soul.

Let your own Will come to pass; let the Divine Will within you shine in
your heart and Soul.

Enlightenment is in Sight, the future is Bright. I Am Divine Light.

Amen

&—&—&—&—&—&—&

En "Lighten" Ment means

E–Enlighten   *N*–Now   *L*–Letting   *I*–Impersonal   *G*–Go   *H*–Healing

T–The   *E*–Essence (Soul)   *N*–Naturally

M–Manage   *E*–Eternal   *N*–Needs   *T*–Today

CAN WE CORRECT OR MODIFY OUR CHOICES?

We must begin where we are and with what we are. We have choices, and we need to walk paths that our choices lead us on for our Soul's Growth and Enlightenment.

Through this and other lifetimes we harbored many belief systems, being controlled or controlling. Most of the time, our Will (Ego) was in control. Before we came into this life, we may have chosen this disease, that specific illness, a certain kind of relationship, etc. Now, if we choose to live in the conventional (convenience) consciousness of medicine, like surgery, chemotherapy, radiation, drug treatment etc., we need to honor and respect that choice.

I previously lived in the conventional (convenience) consciousness, and it served me well at that time; it was for me a dependency consciousness. Now I live in the responsible consciousness.

Yes, we can correct our choices: through a simple process of **Vibrational Energy** change. The remainder of this book describes many ways, tools, circumstances and healing methods with which we can work towards Enlightenment by changing our Vibrational Energy.

Choosing, Allowing, Supporting. The ticket to self empowerment (or Enlightenment) is simply a choice we make. Em Power Ment: in the word Empowerment we find Power, Plan, Prepare, Practice, and Perform. We are only as powerful as our capacity to perceive, receive and use our abilities.

We are born as pure Divine Souls. Now it is time to awaken our Inner Knowing, our Divine Truth.

DIVINE TOOLS FOR SPIRITUAL ENLIGHTENMENT

We wish for a short cut, a quick fix or a magic bullet to ease our way towards Spiritual Enlightenment. But it does not work that way. We need to go through trials and tribulation, through a growth process. These beautiful gifts we receive wake us up and let us acknowledge the Truth within.

Often we bring the Self Healer from within us to the surface. By experiencing unhappiness, we search for happiness. Out of trials and tribulation come learning, and in searching for Truth, we find the God within. To follow a clean, clear life path, we need to know where we were and are, clean up our unfinished business and consciously choose where we need, desire, long to go. Then we can take appropriate steps towards that goal.

֎—֎—֎—֎—֎—֎—֎

Verily, verily, I say unto you,
He that believeth on me, the Works that I do shall he do also;
and greater Works than these shall he do;
because I go unto my Father.
St. John 14:12

A table on the text page lists tools available to us at all times. You may ask your intuition to lead you to tools most important for you at this time in your search for Spiritual Enlightenment. For more information, turn to the page number listed in the first column of the table.

IN WHAT KIND OF ENERGY AM I FUNCTIONING RIGHT NOW?

Before using any of the Divine Tools, ask, "In which of the following energies am I functioning right now?" (We want to be functioning in the Source energy.)

- EGO: our Will, which is society oriented and is society's reality
- ILLUSION: artificial, not real, deception, intended to lead away from the Source
- SOURCE: God, Divine Power, Great Spirit, Creator

THE DIVINE TOOLS DESCRIBED

Page	Divine Tool	Description
9	Dowsing/divining	Using an external indicator (for example, a pendulum) or internal indicator (for example, "gut feel") to detect information that's not available to the ordinary experience of senses of touch, sight, hearing, smell, taste and thought.
12	Being in the present moment and staying centered	Every moment has something to teach us.
13	Divine Principles of Truth	Deeply examine each of thirteen principles. Have you incorporated them in your life?
29	Our energy fields; healing with colors or with other resources	Be aware of energy fields (aura, subtle body, chakras, and meridians) around and within the human system.
42	Our belief system/value system	Examine beliefs that we relate to and get hooked into.
47	Karma and its influences	For every action there is a reaction. Let go of karma that hinders us.
50	Work with influential forces towards our Enlightenment	Examine whether possessions/entities/afflictions/etc. are involved in our life, and let go unwanted influential forces.
60	Psychic senses and other resources	Can discovering your guides or extrasensory abilities enhance your spiritual growth?
66	Soul influences	What is the lesson your Soul chose to learn in this lifetime? Is it beneficial for you to investigate information about level of soul development?
71	Positive life pattern changes	Change one or more aspects of your being—body/physical, emotional, intellectual, mental and spiritual.
75	Life experiences: education, family, finance, relationship, sexual, social, etc.	What can we learn from our experiences in this lifetime?
76	Look at life's blessings	When you have problems with what you feel are bad things, bless the good things in your life.
78	Affirmations	Use affirmations to change what you think and feel. Also use them as prayers of protection.
81	Clean, clearing	Bring radiant Light to one's life, and let go negative emotional energies.
82	Prayers	Petition the Divine Source for help.
84	Meditation	Focus the mind on an object that you choose.
86	Creative visualization	Use imagination to transform yourself.
87	Sacred objects: symbols, dreams, talismans and jewelry	You may feel guided to use a material thing as a reminder of your connection to the Divine Source.
88	Oneness within	Read these inspirational messages.

USING DOWSING AS A TOOL IN YOUR SEARCH

In the search for Spiritual Enlightenment, the art of dowsing/divining is highly useful. When dowsing, you shift into a neutral-minded or meditative state to open to all possibilities; the shift allows you to quickly assess a variety of approaches, then find one that matches your needs at the time. Thus, we use dowsing/divining as a way to heal ourselves.

The shortened description, below, of the dowsing/divining technique is taken from the booklet *Dowsing/Divining*. If you need further elaboration, refer to the Bibliography for books by Anneliese and Doris Hagemann.

WHAT IS DOWSING/DIVINING?

It is an ancient art, known in and used before biblical times. Each civilization has a way to tune into a Higher Consciousness for answers about Past, Present and Future.

With dowsing/divining, one tunes into a Higher Consciousness by first asking a question then receiving, via a dowsing tool, a response that would not be available via our typical experience of the senses of sight, hearing, smell, taste, touch and thinking (trying to figure things out). The tool by which you receive a response is a personal choice; see "Dowsing/Divining Tools," below, for examples.

Albert Einstein said, "*I know very well that many scientists consider Dowsing as a type of ancient superstition. According to my conviction this is, however, unjustified. The Dowsing rod is a simple instrument which shows the reaction of the human nervous system to certain factors which are unknown to us at this time.*"

The American Dowser Quarterly Digest, Spring 1997.

Why do we desire (choose) to dowse?

- To be Enlightened.
- To stay Healthy, Happy and live in Harmony on All Levels of Our Total Being from now on and forever forward.

DOWSING/DIVINING TOOLS

A dowsing device can be an instrument external to the body, for example, dowsing rods or a pendulum. Or, one's body and its sensations can be the instrument, for example, a personal sense of intuition, gut feelings, body movements, finger stick, kinesiology (muscle checking), etc.

GUIDELINES FOR DOWSING

First, ask whether you are functioning in the Source energy, as described on page 7 in "In What Kind of Energy Am I Functioning Right Now?" Next, please look over and use the following guidelines. At step 11, below, frame your question. For example, you could dowse through the list of Divine Tools on page 8; ask if using a specific tool at this time is for your Highest Good in your Search for Spiritual Enlightenment.

1.	**Protect yourself.** You may use a prayer such as "God Force surrounds me with White Light and Golden Light," or whatever affirmation or prayer of protection feels right to you.
2.	**Let go of Ego.** On a piece of paper write first your Name. Then write "I let go of Ego, I embrace God (or Goddess, Universe, Spirit), I channel the truth."
	You may need to write, "I let go Ego" more than once because our Ego (self Will) likes to control our Soul. Or else write, "I let go Ego. 5X" or "I let go Ego. 10X" where 5X or 10X signifies the number of repetitions of the phrase "I let go Ego." Or write, "Dear Egos, please communicate from the sacred space of Truth, work with the Divine Vibration, and let go all materialistic attachments and tendencies."
3.	**Clean, clear your dowsing tool.** Blow on, rub, or talk to your dowsing tool to remove extraneous energies or influences that might interfere with the tool's ability to clearly indicate an answer.
4.	**Find your "Yes," your "No," your "Neutral."** Ask questions one at a time of your dowsing/divining tool in order to learn how it responds when the answer is Yes, No, or Neutral. A Neutral indication means "neither Yes nor No." Ask a question, then immediately ask yourself, "I wonder what the answer is?" in order to have an impartial attitude and to not let the Ego influence the way the tool responds.
	To find your Yes, No and Neutral, you can ask the dowsing tool to respond to questions whose answers you already know. For example, the tool responds Yes when you ask the question, "Is my name *<your own first and last name>*?" It responds No to the question "Is my name Groucho X?" It responds Neutral to "Please give me a strong neutral response."
5.	**Use the word Suppress.** Write the word **Suppress** on the piece of paper where you wrote your **Name** and the phrase "I let go of Ego." Hold the paper on you when you dowse. You may have to write the word **Suppress** more than once. Suppress means pulling your energy closer to you, especially when you are in a group of people and experiencing **Interference**.
6.	**Set up conditions so your being can receive an answer.** Drink plenty of water (an energy conductor). You may need fresh air, food, or a walk.
7.	**Breath through your mouth, do not block your natural flow of energy.** Put your tongue behind your top front teeth, to stay grounded to Mother Earth.

(continued on the next page)

(continued from the previous page)

8.	**Ask permission to dowse. May I?** Do I have permission on all levels of my consciousness (and, if another person is involved, all levels of their consciousness)? Levels of consciousness are **Conscious, Subconscious, Superconscious, Unconscious, Dupi,** and **Soul**. (Dupi means to link up, reintegrate, and unite to the archetype, to the good/God, to the original pattern, to open the door.)
9.	**Ask permission to dowse. Can I?** Do I have the ability to successful dowse in this area?
10.	**Ask permission to dowse. Should I?** Is it for the above Highest Good of All concerned to dowse in this area?
11.	**Ask one question at a time, and be very specific.** You must phrase the question so it can be answered with a Yes or a No movement. (There are other movements you may experience, such as "I Don't know," "Not at this Time," "Don't ask this question.") The key to getting an accurate, reliable response is to use specific, on-target words when you phrase the question.
12.	**Be thankful for guidance received.** And show your Gratitude.

Practice, practice. And remember the K.I.S. principle—Keep it Simple.

IDEAS AND QUESTIONS YOU MAY CHOOSE TO CONSIDER AND PRESENT TO YOUR DOWSING TOOL

- Is this question appropriate to ask?
- Is asking this question advisable?
- Is this the most accurate set of words to use in the question?
- Is this the most beneficial question? Is this the right question?
- Is this answer the Truth?
- Is acting on this response for my/others' above Highest Good?
- Is there another way I need to ask the question?
- Do I need to look for different ways of Enlightenment?
- What does my Soul truly need to fulfill its Commitment/Mission?

I wish you guidance and success on your journey of the Inner Art of Dowsing, the Golden Key to Tapping Energies. Bless Love.

Anneliese Gabriel Hagemann

BEING IN THE PRESENT MOMENT AND STAYING CENTERED

Are we living in Health, Happiness and Harmony within the Divine Source? If the answer is "No," we may ask the Divine Source (Creative Energy, God, Goddess, Universe) to come take permanent occupancy within us. The Divine is the Truth.

Our goal is to stay centered by living totally in the Now, in the Truth. Give service in the Now. Always stay in the present moment.

⚭—⚭—⚭—⚭—⚭—⚭—⚭

Walking my Path of Enlightenment, I receive info from unexpected sources. It is so exciting to be on this planet called Earth right now. The overriding questions I get are "Where are we Now?" and "What are we doing with the Now?" I received these two messages:

REMEMBERING YOUR HIGHER SOUL SELF

Come on, my children: open your eyes and let the Sun/Son of the spirit come in.

Have you heard the heavenly music which connects you to the rhythm of your Soul? Have you heard me calling you? Pick up your staff and follow me. Be ready to explore the unknown.

My children, I love you. Don't you remember when I held you in my arms, when I cradled you, because you where afraid to come to Earth?

You are here now, so enjoy every moment. It has much to teach you about honor and respect, Unconditional Love, about surrendering to me. Are you afraid to give up your Ego, your Will? Are you allowing your Ego to be in control instead of me, your Higher Soul Self?

Wake up, come smell the roses, and see the beauty in every flower. The flower is you; have you forgotten?   June 13, 2000

⚭—⚭—⚭—⚭—⚭—⚭—⚭

FULFILLMENT IS IN THE NOW

Believe you are special, that you are made in the Image of God, a Pure Light Being.

Our Walk of Enlightenment is of Eternal Truth and Unconditional Love.

By being a Pure Light Being, we obey and adhere (devote ourselves) to Divine Principles of Truth.

DIVINE PRINCIPLES OF TRUTH

The Mountaintop, or the Summit as it may be called, may be viewed from the North, East, South or West; from above, below, or from within. Each view looks different; yet each viewer looks at the same Mountaintop. So it is with religions of man—Buddhism, Christianity, Confucianism, Hinduism, Islam, Judaism, Taoism, and so forth. Each created its own principles that follow some of the Divine Principles of Truth. In the end, it all comes back to the Relationship of "THE ONE GOD WITHIN."

In our life, each of us searches for Truth within our heart. Read through the following Divine Principles, and carefully consider each one. How do they apply to you right now in your life? To what degree have you incorporated each one?

PRINCIPLE #1. UNCONDITIONAL LOVE

Chakra

The Heart chakra is where the energy of Unconditional Love manifests.

Unconditional Love: what does it mean?

Unconditional Love is true Love, Divine Love, God's Love in our Heart and Soul. Unconditional Love for all Creation means:

- Honor, respect, patience, hope, tolerance, kindness, truth, trust, joy, peace and consistency.
- To love unconditionally is to love not limited by any terms or conditions; it's absolute, unreserved, the Infinite.
- Be a living example to all we meet, living in the energy of Bless Love (God's Love).
- To me it means loving each and every one without Condition, also honoring, respecting each individual for who and where they are in their lives.

Humanity recreated God in its own image to fulfill its identity needs. So remember, it is important that how we see "Divinity" is how we see ourselves. Do you see yourself as Unconditional Love? Conditional Love is part of the process of learning how to express Unconditional Love. Conditional Love implies fear, separation and issues of self-worth. Unconditional Love expresses without judgment, limitation or expectation. Unconditional Love is the state of being in which we naturally reside if all beliefs and expectations are put aside. Conditional love is attachment. Unconditional Love is freedom. Both play major parts in how relationships unfold. (See "Principle #2. Honest Feelings and Knowing Them.")

Using the Inner Art of Dowsing in the Search for My Spiritual Enlightenment

All paths eventually lead to Oneness. Wearing another being's shoes tells you their feelings and story. I am another you.

THREE BLOSSOMS OF LOVE

From the root of Love, God grew three blossoms: to love God, to love yourself and to love your neighbor. If one of these is impaired, the others are also impaired.

CHOOSE LOVE OR FEAR

Love frees us. Fear freezes us.

When I get out of my way, I get on my way.

Love is Magic—God and me in creation.

PRINCIPLE #2. HONEST FEELINGS AND KNOWING THEM

Chakra

Either the Solar Plexus chakra or Heart chakra is where the energy of honest feelings manifests.

Honesty: what does it mean?

When you speak or listen to someone, or think about something, and you have this strange gut feeling, or heart pounding, it might be telling you this is not right—something is wrong.

Honor it as your Truth. It is your Inner Knowing, your Instinct. Listen to it, act on it.

I often feel it when I am on the phone with someone. If I allow the other person to overstep my Energy field boundaries, it is my issue. Then, using the Bless Love Vibration (say "Bless Light, Bless Love" repeatedly) is a wonderful tool to balance the Energy.

When we are honest we live in Truth—a state of being true. Here we can live and embody trust within ourselves. It implies that you are faithful, loyal, exact, correct, right.

Honesty creates integrity within yourself, and you find that it becomes a potent force that you do not desire to relinquish.

Are you ready to explore your Inner Core? It is not what's in front of us that stops us; it is what's inside of us.

Be honest about your emotions; ask, "How do I feel?" Acknowledge those "gut feelings," your intuition. Be aware not only of your external surroundings, but also of your inner dynamics. Don't just "live in your head." You may need to look at an emotion and evaluate what to do with it. For example, you could accept the feeling, then let it go.

The Truth sets us free: our senses take in all the data; next, the mind formulates a thought about the sensation; then our brain produces a biochemical reaction in the body; finally, we experience the data as a feeling—an emotion like compassion, sympathy, anger, frustration, and so forth.

Honesty in Our Relationships

The material about relationships may seem out of place, but it was felt to be vital to include it in this section. We must carefully consider relationships before moving on.

Relationships are a vital key in the process of spiritual growth. We do not function alone in this physical realm, but are interconnected with all beings, with all things. And honesty is a vital component in life. Thus, we regard honesty with respect to three different relationships, which also overlap:

- One's relationship with God
- One's relationship with oneself
- One's relationship with others

Relating to God

If we do not recognize our connection to God (or whatever we call our Higher Power), we interfere with our destiny.

Do you pay only lip service to the Divine—like a child forced to go to church? Do you mouth, without feeling or conviction, prayers and songs, meditations and what not? How honest is that?

REIGN TOGETHER

Let your Soul speak. Let it express the beauty, the joy of living with me in the highest realm of eternity.

I have the answer. You only need to ask.

Are you afraid of me—the true You, the Source, the Guide, the Light?

Come, stay open, and let me reign with you in eternal beauty.

Amen.

HAROLD IS MY NAME

The Christmas carol "Hark, the Herald Angels sing, Glory to the Newborn King" came into my consciousness when I received the following message.

It is you I created, in the Image of Me. The God "Harold" is my Name. The newborn King is you, my Child, an Angel living on Earth, to help lift the Consciousness and Awareness of being One with me. Have you forgotten?

Most of you have forgotten where you came from. You are me, and I am you; all the things I do, you can do also. Have Faith, live the Truth, the True Light Embodiment, and everything works in the wonderment of Oneness.

Come, in the midst of all Creation, I have prepared a place for you. Claim it, and it is yours forever.

Amen,
Your Lord Harold

SOURCE AND GOD

Source is bigger than God. God is the Creator of Creation.

God is the Shell of the Source, and in the Shell lies the Core of Creative Vibration with our internal net connection.

ON THE PATH

He who heeds instruction is on the Path of Life and Truth.

He who walks in integrity walks securely.

Using the Inner Art of Dowsing in the Search for My Spiritual Enlightenment

☙—☙—☙—☙—☙—☙—☙

Trust in the Lord with all your heart, and do not rely on your own insight. In all your ways acknowledge him and he makes straight your path.

Proverbs 3:5–6

☙—☙—☙—☙—☙—☙—☙

Teach me to do thy Will, for thou art my God: thy spirit is good; lead me into the land of uprightness.

Psalm 143:10

☙—☙—☙—☙—☙—☙—☙

ALWAYS MY PROTECTOR

God is my security guard, always on the job. Thank you, dear Lord, for being our security guard. Always protecting us is truly a big job.

Relating to Oneself

Honesty with oneself is often one of the most difficult relationships to work with. We are very adept at hiding from ourselves. We keep thoughts running wildly so that we are not certain about what we are feeling or thinking. Finding that honesty with yourself might seem a difficult task. Perhaps the best way to put it is to say that when you are honest with yourself, you are at peace with yourself. You do not feel a need to rush about and rationalize every thought and feeling. You do not feel the need to run away and hide. You are calm and willing to sit with yourself on a mountainside and just be, tranquil of mind and with a quiet consciousness.

Some key words to ponder when you ask the question, "Where am I with myself?"

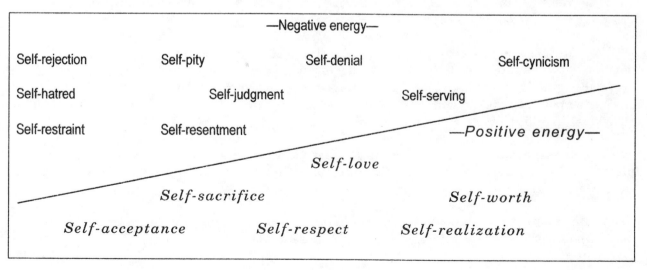

Using the Inner Art of Dowsing in the Search for My Spiritual Enlightenment

 END THE MASQUERADE

It does not matter what symbol we carry or under which star we were born. It matters that we carry the staff of Truth and are connected to the Source.

The external is a facade we wear so no one recognizes our inner flaws. We do not like to be shamed, harassed or be put down. So, in front of everyone we masquerade, made up of elegant clothes, lipstick, and jewelry or shirts, shoes, boats and cars so not to be seen as we need to be seen.

When we truly face our job head on, we look beyond the external.

The true Source is God. Hold it tied deep in your heart, and let the outside world depart.

Amen.

Relating to Others

Primary in your relationship with another person is the fact that you must have an honest relationship with yourself before you can have a healthy relationship with another. That is not to say that two people cannot work on building and improving themselves through a sharing and reflective relationship.

In one way or another, all relationships affect your growth process. Be aware of who you choose to be with, work with, socialize with, party with, etc. When examining honesty within your relationships with others (be they spouse, partner, boss, sibling, child, friend, etc.), be aware of how you interact with others. How far will you go to control someone, or to what degree will you let someone control you? Are you submissive or dominating? Do you use passive aggression; do they?

For yourself and others, it is best, when able, to strive for healing relationships. That is, develop relationships that help elevate each other and encourage individual growth. (Read "Principle #1. Unconditional Love" in the preceding section.) A relationship of a higher level supports openness and provides freedom to be true to yourself and to others. That kind of relationship is nurturing and helpful but not smothering.

As you enter and leave relationships, realize that we all are part of the oneness of the universe. We all strive in one way or another to better understand ourselves and that connection to the universe.

Another point: examine your ideas about gender and sex. We are all "bisexual" beings, made up of both sexes—sperm and egg, male and female. Each of us embodies an equal and vast potential.

Relationships between men and women must be mutually respectful. Neither gender is better than the other. Respect and acceptance of each other as individuals, each with their own thoughts, values, beliefs, etc., is a necessity.

Do not place wildly ambitious expectations on any relationship unless it is the one between yourself and the Divine Source. Relationships with other people should be taken out of the fairy tale realm; there is no Prince Charming, and there is no Sleeping Beauty. No one but you can wake you up or save you from the dragon.

There are many types and colors of humans. We judge each human by their intellect, their accomplishments, their appearance and their clothes. Do we have the right to judge them? We are all created equals in God's Image.

&—&—&—&—&—&—&

IMAGE OF GOD: WHAT DOES IT MEAN?

What does the Image of God mean to us?

To me, when I look at someone, I see nothing but the purity of their Soul, the image of God, the Beauty, the Divine. For me there is no judgment, for do I have the right to do so?

As I judge so I am judged, and this no longer serves me in my life now.

We are Divine Creations, and it is our duty to accept the Divine in everyone we meet.

The image of "God" is not magic, and the Bible is not magic. When we quote things, it is not enough either. We need to live it from the inside out, being responsible for our deeds and living in the truth of our Divinity. That is when changes take place inside us.

&—&—&—&—&—&—&

JUDGE NOT: VERSES FROM ST. MATTHEW

Judge not, that you be not judged. *St. Matthew 7:1*

For with what judgment you judge, you will be judged; and with the measure you use, it will be measured back to you. *St. Matthew 7:2*

And why do you look at the speck in your brother's eye, but do not consider the plank in your own eye? *St. Matthew 7:3*

&—&—&—&—&—&—&

Do not judge or ridicule anyone until you have walked in their shoes.

Using the Inner Art of Dowsing in the Search for My Spiritual Enlightenment

PRINCIPLE #3. NON-INTERFERENCE

We all like to help others: we <u>want</u> them to feel better; <u>want</u> them to not experience the difficulties we did; we <u>want</u> to protect them, especially our close family and friends.

<u>Want</u> is our <u>EGO</u>, our <u>Will</u> interference; we allow it to control ourselves and others. Do we have the right to do so?

We need to ask ourselves, "Is it for the above Highest Good of all concerned for me to get involved, to give advice, to assist, to take life's lessons away thereby creating new karma for ourselves and others, to judge, to control, and to fix everything?"

A little example: After our younger daughter had her first child, I stayed with her. I was giving her advice that she was not ready for, without her asking me for it. My daughter got very upset with me. A few days later when I was back in our home, I received a message from God that said, "Let your daughter experience her own Motherhood." I told her what I received, and she said, "See, Mom." I apologized, and from then on everything was back to normal. I learned an important lesson there.

Here's another little story. I was at someone's home, and a lady had a soda in her hand. I said to her, "This is not good for you." Another woman, standing next to me, said, "Did Carol ask you for advice?" I replied, "No." Again, I was judging and speaking out of control.

How do I know what is good or not good for the other person? Always ask your intuition two questions, "Do I have my permission to comment or speak on this subject?" and "Does the other person give me permission to comment or speak on this subject?"

PRINCIPLE #4. REALIZATION OF CAUSE AND EFFECT. ACTION-REACTION

What we think, speak and do, whether with positive or negative intention, affects us and others.

Each word, symbol or number used in thought, deed, speech, writing, etc. gives off a Vibration. Using them, we create Energies; we send them out, and they return to us a thousandfold.

Be very careful about contents of our thoughts and to whom we project them. Remember the energy comes back to us as fast as we send it out. Thoughts create our Reality in the next moment. Words can heal or steal our Life. We are in control of words, and they are our tools.

So master the Words. Words tell our Life story. Words are our communication tools.

When we say, "I can't," "I am afraid," "I am no good," "I am tired," etc., our Subconscious picks it up and believes it, and then we manifest it.

Heal Thyself with words and thoughts. I do it all the time; it is simple, fast, easy and everlasting. I make positive Statements, Affirmations, Prayers, and Meditations. For examples, see "Affirmations," "Meditation" and "Index to Messages."

There is no need for suffering. It begins with surrendering our attitudes.

By no longer fighting the Divine Principles of Truth, we live them. It means staying with and applying those Divine Principles in our lives, without stress, enjoying Peace, Truth, Harmony, etc. Living the Divine Principles is living in the Purpose of our life; the choice is always ours.

&—&—&—&—&—&—&

Keep moving on in the Forever Vibration.

PRINCIPLE #5. NATURAL ORDER. ORIGIN-SOURCE

"Natural order" means absence of confusion or disturbance, that from which anything primarily proceeds.

We as human beings need to let Nature do its work.

We take from our planet Earth without permission anything we want, and put back our polluted stuff (garbage). Do we have that right? How long do we think Mother Earth can handle it?

Recognize you are part of the Natural Order

and have an obligation to keep it flowing for all.

When we take from it, we take from ALL!

MOTHER EARTH CRIES OUT

As Mother Earth is crying out, dying out, overflowing in some places,
drying out in others, producing eruptions of mountains,
hurricanes and earthquakes,
She is saying,
"Are you on your path? Have you taken care of me?
I have fed you and cradled you; I gave you water, everything I have.
What have you done? You've taken from me, not given back.
Your attitude is 'me, me, me.'

Wake up, my children.
Honor and respect yourself and me, and we truly can live in Harmony."

Yours truly, Mother Earth

Gaia = Earth Mother Goddess.

We human beings can begin to function as the Planetary Nervous System for Gaia, working in harmony with the Organism.

Humanity is a part of Nature. Life depends on the uninterrupted functioning of the natural system that ensures our supply of energy and nutrients. Civilization is rooted in Nature, which has shaped human culture and influenced all artistic and scientific achievement. And living in harmony with Nature gives man the best opportunities for developing his creativity, for rest and for recreation.

PRINCIPLE #6. PATIENCE

"Patience" is the quality of being patient; the quality of quietness and calmness in waiting for something to happen; persevering.

In the Western world, we <u>want</u> (ego-based) results, such as Enlightenment, immediately—today. But it takes work, one step at a time, before we reach our heart's and Soul's goal—Spiritual Enlightenment.

Again, without patience, we <u>want</u> (ego-based) the tomorrow immediately—today.

Patience is living in the Moment, in the Now.

I know it is easy to lose patience with a child, partner, parent, coworker, clerk at the check out counter, and so forth, because we are always in a hurry.

What are we so hurried about? Is it to make money to buy (which is an illusion) happiness, or to buy extra things we truly do not need or to keep up with the Jones's? Is it because we feel we miss something, like a TV program?

Do we fear that we are missing tomorrow? But have we truly lived today? We may need to ask this of ourselves.

Patience is living in God's Divine Truth, in his everlasting Joy, Peace and Harmony, and not expecting happiness from material things you buy. God's Universal Love is free, and it is without condition—there are no monthly payments, no interest due.

All you need to do is ask the Divine to be in you forever, and you experience the most bazaar, peaceful feeling you can ever imagine. You love it.

Patience has rewards. What is mine to work with comes to me. Knowing that is good medicine. I trust that God provides his work for me. I work in the energy of wholeness.

PRINCIPLE #7. RESPONSIBILITY

"Responsibility," what a big word it is. It certainly holds a lot of energy for us. What does it mean?

- To answer, to reply, also being accountable, answerable
- A trust or the like, resting on a person's ability to answer in payment

When we commit to a task, it is then our responsibility to obey it and work with it.

Responsibility also means when we sign a contract, if it is a marriage vow (a solemn promise, an oath made to God), a land contract, or any kind of contract, we are then responsible to fulfill it.

By accepting responsibility, we acknowledge our ability to respond.

Knowledge is a treasure, but practicing responsibility is the key to it.

We think it is hard to be responsible for our own progress. We seek someone to carry us and put us on a higher level. We must understand that progress is based on our effort and that responsibility goes with it.

The world is not a burden. We make it a burden by our wants and desires, with our thoughts and perceptions of things. When these are removed, the world is as light as a feather.

We are responsible for future generations. Whatever we do today affects all generations to come. Every thought we have and every decision we make affects tomorrow's world; so we need to be brave and look at ourselves. Is this what we want/desire for our children?

We need to heal ourselves, so we can relate to our children. These children come to this earthly plane with a very high Vibration. We adults have a hard time relating to them, and they to us. However, if we value ourselves as spiritual beings and abide by Divine Principles of Truth, we should have no problem communicating with these beautiful beings of Love and Light.

There is a reason for every season in our realm of experiences.

PRINCIPLE #8. PROGRESSION=ADVANCE

"Progression" means

* A movement, proceeding onward in your growth
* Increase in Light and Knowledge
* To improve, go towards perfection, move forward on your journey of Enlightenment

Never sit still. Always be open-minded. If you feel a need to take more classes, do it. If you feel a need to read more books, do it. If you feel a need to be in touch with cards, Angels, animals, Spirit Guides, or stones to learn from or with, do it.

The responsibility is yours, no one else's, so walk through the Gate of Enlightenment. The Doors are all open; are you ready to step through them? When you've stepped through, look for opportunities to share your beautiful gifts of Enlightenment with others.

PRINCIPLE #9. ONENESS

"Oneness" means

* Living in Oneness with God/Universe, Nature, and every human being
* Closely United, forming a Whole, Undivided, in Union, All One

It does not matter who we are—the colors we wear; the religion in which we participate; the country in which we live; or the culture with which we identify. We are all One, created by God in his own Image. Be also aware that all existence is part of the Oneness.

The state of Being one with the All, we may call it Paradise.

To live in Oneness again is our Goal, living in shining Light for our Soul.

FIVE RULES TO BE HAPPY

1. Free your heart from hatred.
2. Free your mind from worry.
3. Live simply.
4. Expect less.
5. Give more.

Ki Dragon, also known as Weiming, a 22-year old male from Singapore

Using the Inner Art of Dowsing in the Search for My Spiritual Enlightenment

PRINCIPLE #10. FORGIVENESS=TO GIVE UP RESENTMENT

"Forgiveness" means

* To pardon, to free from a claim or from the consequences
* To err is human, to forgive is Divine
* The act of forgiving yourself and others

By letting go the Past, you step through the Doorway now to reclaim your Power (Enlightenment).

When you forgive yourself and others, you may be amazed how free you feel. Experience it, and you feel free. Every time you forgive, you already feel lighter. Then live in harmony with yourself and others.

FORGIVENESS PRAYER

Thank you, Father/Mother God, for everything that has happened to me,
whether it was painful or pleasurable.
It made me the I Am that I am now.

I forgive you, *<name>*, for all the things you have done to me.
Please forgive me, *<name>*, for all the thing I did to you.
Let us live in peace and harmony forever.

PRINCIPLE #11. SERVING: BEING A SERVANT FOR GOD/UNIVERSE/PLANET EARTH/MANKIND

Service is to perform regular or continuous duties in behalf of God, being in God's Employment. Here are some examples:

- Assistance, kindness, rendering to another, to work for, to promote, to be of use, to administer, to manage, to answer a purpose, to answer your Call from above.
- To render Spiritual obedience and worship.
- Serving as a volunteer. It could be the Red Cross, a hospice program, peer counseling, serving in a church, membership in a Chamber of Commerce, as a Brother/Sister program. There are many organizations that could use our service.

Are you ready for it?

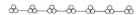

PAVE THE WAY FOR EACH OTHER

As you serve the Will of God, you meet beautiful people from around the World, all of them Souls looking for Enlightenment.

Why not pave the way with Unconditional Love, Honor, Respect, Truth and Joy in your Heart?

Amen.

PRINCIPLE #12. DETACHMENT: DETACHING FROM THE OUTCOME

"Detachment" means

- To separate, to disengage, to loosen, to unfasten, to remove, to part from, to stand apart
- Sent on a separate service
- To separate for a special purpose or service, especially Divine Service

I am detached from the outcome; I am free to serve the Thee, God, Goddess, Universe.

You are not responsible for the way others feel or react. With Unconditional Love and for the Highest Good, do what you need to do. Then step back from your work when it is finished.

Principle #13. Surrendering to the Creator of All

"Surrender" means to give up oneself, to yield to the power of another. To me, the "other" is God. Give up my Will for God's Will/Divine Will.

Do your work by surrendering to God. Don't think that you are helping others; instead, think that God is helping them, taking you as his instrument.

If everything else fails, here is a prayer.

Prayer of Surrender

Dearest God, Cosmic Source from whom I have come, I, *<your name>*, this day, at this moment, return to you my Will and my being. I surrender my life, my future, my goals, my plans, my hopes, and my fears to Your Divine Plans for me.

I dedicate myself to placing You first in my life. I surrender all that I am, and all that I have, past, present and future, to Your service, without limits, without stipulation or condition. Grant that my greatest desire is to love and serve You completely.

If I wander from this resolve, gently strengthen me. If I am hesitant in letting go, gently encourage me. You, who are Love itself, bless my commitment to make You first in my life. And now having given all, let my emptiness be filled with Your Presence. Amen

Quoted with permission of the author, Pastor Thomas Sherbrook,
in the church bulletin of Sunday, September 17, 2000 for
St. Ann's Church and Healing Sanctuary,
5933 West National Ave.
West Allis, WI 53214

OUR ENERGY FIELDS; HEALING WITH COLOR OR WITH OTHER RESOURCES

There exist numerous definitions and approaches to dealing with or describing energy fields around and within the human system. Awareness of the following energy fields/systems (described in more detail, below) may enhance your growth and striving toward Enlightenment.

- Subtle body
- Aura
- Chi energy and meridians
- Colors of the aura and chakras
- Chakras

SUBTLE BODY

One definition of the energy field is the subtle body (nonphysical psychic body) that is superimposed on our physical body. It contains the more spiritual parts of our being. It is measured as an electromagnetic force field. (Kirlian photography has produced photographic images of it.)

One's aura is the external manifestation of the subtle body.

Chakras are manifestations of the subtle body in the core of the physical body.

AURA

The Soul surrounds the aura (this is what Anneliese feels).

The aura is often referred to as surrounding the lower bodies with a force field of energy on which impressions, thoughts, feelings, words and actions of the individual and other individuals are registered. Some scientists have referred to this as the L-field, which they think controls manifestation of the physical body.

The aura continually vibrates and changes size and shape. People sensitive to auras also note a variety of colors flowing around and within the aura. Different colors and locations denote different goings on or aspects of the person, their health, mental balances, consciousness, etc. Many people have the ability to see the aura (energy field) around the body. In fact, all people can do so if they relax, slightly blur their eyes and not get too tense in their focus.

Integrity of the aura can affect the body. If the aura is unbalanced, the body may be left open to illness. Energy may be transferred from one person's aura to another either intentionally or unintentionally. By visualization and auric exercises, one may enhance and strengthen one's aura.

CHI ENERGY AND MERIDIANS

There are numerous energy flows, lines, vortices, and centers in and around the body. Awareness of these areas helps one tune into problems or issues. There may be a blockage or energy flow problem that needs to be addressed and treated to encourage better health.

Chi (sometimes spelled "Qi") is a Chinese word for a concept about energy found throughout the universe. It is a form of vital energy verging on being both matter and energy. The proper flow or balance of this energy in the body is important for the body to be in health.

Meridians are pathways for the flow of Chi energy. Meridians are found in the human body and have been measured electronically, thematically, and via radioactivity. Acupressure and acupuncture points are found along these meridians, (The science of acupuncture has been a part of Chinese culture and civilization for thousands of years.) Fourteen major meridians interconnect in various body organs and parts.

When energy flow is unrestricted, the body harmonizes the flow to keep it functioning well. Stress and other problems may hamper the flow (overloading the circuit).

Pressure on, massaging, or passing hands over the meridians may help stabilize the flow. For more information about meridians and ways to use them to bring about better health, consult a book by John F. Thie, ©1994 *Touch for Health* (see the Bibliography).

AURA AND CHAKRA COLORS, CHAKRAS AND THEIR MEANINGS FOR HEALING

Listed in the next section are colors that may be found in the aura and may also relate to chakras. Also, varying shades, muddiness, clarity and other aspects of the colors imply different states associated with our chakras.

The concept of chakras has been found in cultures and in many belief systems in India for thousands of years. Chakras are described as vortices through which energy flows both in and out of the body. The power or energy that is involved with chakras comes from Kundalini or evolutionary energy and from a spiritual force within. Chakras are to be found on all layers and levels (spiritual, physical, mental, emotional, auric, etc.).

There are seven main chakras and more than 100 chakras located all over the body.

A person's development influences which chakras are predominant. Some people have too much energy located in lower chakras (which are the Root, Sex and Solar Plexus chakras), leaving the central and upper chakras weak. Other people overemphasize upper chakras, leaving lower chakras weak. Chakras must have balanced energy flows. Neglect of one aspect of the self does not bring balance or harmony, but produces an imbalance that might open a person to a variety of problems.

Interaction with people has a great effect on one's chakras. Some people unconsciously pull energy from another's open or unguarded chakras. When we interact with or are merely in another's presence, our chakras react to that person. Awareness of this is helpful in understanding why one might feel drained, invigorated, uncomfortable and so forth around particular people.

Much information is becoming available regarding chakras, their clearing, unblocking, opening and developing. Often it is helpful to focus on, wear, hold or use colors associated with various chakras to enhance or help function of chakras. It has been noted that humming or singing some of the musical notes mentioned below may also help to clear or stimulate the various chakras.

Again we suggest you consult reading material or specialists if you need more information or help with chakras or the aura. A few interesting books are listed below and are listed in topics that follow; see the Bibliography for names of publishers.

- Reuben Amber, ©1991 *Color Therapy*
- Barbara Bowers, ©1989 *What Color Is Your Aura?*
- Dan Dupuis and Richard Krull, ©1992 *Creating Your Light Body*
- Richard Gerber, ©2000 *A Practical Guide to Vibrational Medicine*
- Ambika Wauters, ©1997 *Chakras and Their Archetypes* and ©1998 *Healing with the Energy of the Chakras*

Descriptions of Aura and Chakra Colors, Chakras and Their Associated Foci, Glands, Musical Notes, Symbols, Metals, Foods, Stones, Plants and Animals for Healing and Balancing Our Physical, Emotional, Mental, Spiritual, and Soul Being

You may use your dowsing method to learn which colors, chakras and attributes below are most important for you to investigate to balance your physical, emotional, mental, spiritual and Soul Being at this time.

Red. Root Chakra

Attribute	Characteristics associated with the Root chakra or the color red
Focus	Physical. Life force, Oneness, Grounding.
Related colors	Reds, crimson, scarlet, fire.
	Cosmic color Red is the element of fire, relates to our sight (eyes).
	The positive vibration of red relates to and resembles Blood—the symbol of life, strength, vitality, and power.
	It also embodies the energies of trust, dynamism, employ, encouragement, enfold, knowing, choosing, stability, Godly, Lord, peace, survival, virile, materialistic, passionate, hatred, revenge.
Glands	Adrenals
Musical note	C
Symbol	Triangle means "Trinity." The triangle may be used as **protection** over the Root chakra.
Metals	Related to the color red are iron, rubidium, titanium, bismuth, zinc, copper.
Foods (vegetables, fruit, herbs, spices)	Related to the color red are eggplant, meat, onions, pepper, red beets, radishes, red cabbage, tomato, watercress, most deep-red-skinned fruits (such as cherries, cranberries, red currants, red plums, strawberries, watermelon, yams, rhubarb and other red-skinned fruits and vegetables). Cayenne pepper.
	The following authors' books might also be helpful (see the Bibliography):
	• Hanna Kroeger, ©1995 *Spices to the Rescue.*
	• Mary Summer Rain, ©1990 *Earthway.*
	• Jethro Kloss, ©1995 *Back to Eden.*
	• John Lust, ©1974 *The Herb Book.*
	• Steven Foster and James A. Duke, ©1990 *Peterson Field Guide Series: A Field Guide to Medicinal Plants, Eastern and Central North America.*

(continued on the next page)

(continued from the previous page)

Stones	Some of the stones related to the color of red are carnelian bixbite, cobaltite, chalcedony, copal, crocoite, cuprite, granite, gypsum, grossular garnet, halite, inesite, jasper, opal, quartz (red phantom), rhodochrosite, ruby, rutile, spinel, tantalite, topaz, zincite.
	Books authored by Melody, ©1991 *Love is in the Earth, a Kaleidoscope of Crystals* and ©1993, *Love is in the Earth, Mineralogical Pictorial* might be helpful, or check for other books at your public library.
Plants (trees, flowers, etc.)	Related to the color red are red maple, red cedar, North American juniper, red pine, Scotch or Norway pine, redwood in California.
	The following authors' books might also be helpful (see the Bibliography):
	• Allen J. Coombes, ©1992 *DK Handbooks: Trees.*
	• Steven Foster and James A. Duke, ©1990 *Peterson Field Guide Series: A Field Guide to Medicinal Plants, Eastern and Central North America.*
	• Ellen Evert Hopman, ©1992 *Tree Medicine Tree Magic.*
	• Frank D. Venning and Saito C. Manabuo, ©1984 *Wild Flowers of North America: A Guide to Field Identification.*
Animals	The following authors' books might be helpful (see the Bibliography):
	• Ted Andrews, ©1993 *Animal-Speak, The Spiritual and Magical Powers of Creatures Great and Small.*
	• John Bull and John Farrand, Jr., ©1977 *The Audubon Society: Field Guide to North American Birds, Eastern Region.*
	• Miklos Udvardy, ©1977 *The Audubon Society: Field Guide to North American Birds, Western Region.*
	• John O. Whitaker, ©1980 *The Audubon Society: Field Guide to North American Mammals.*
Other	There may be another attribute for you to explore.

Orange. Sex Chakra

Attribute	Characteristics associated with the Sex chakra or the color orange
Focus	Emotional creativity center of our being, sacred—holy, physical creativity, interest.
Related colors	Red-orange. **Cosmic color Orange is the element of water and relates to taste (tongue).**
Glands	Ovaries, prostate, testicles.
Musical note	D.
Symbol	Rectangle means "Opportunity," Life Force. Use the rectangle as **protection** over the Sex chakra. Health, vitality, vital force, soul of energy, live wire. Domination of others through force of vital qualities. Position of responsibility. Easier to rule then to serve. Usually well-balanced. It is an expression of wisdom and reasoning powers. Other positive vibrations relating to the color orange are acceptance, acquit, attuned, clearing, climbing, collected, delightful, elated, frugal, Godly, knowing thyself, in time, precious, surprise, transition, wonder. Freedom from limitations, also new ideas, in the here and now, social, health.
Metals	Relating to the color of orange are selenium, iron, calcium, nickel, zinc, rubidium, and manganese.
Foods (vegetables, fruit, herbs, spices)	Oranges, apricots, carrot, peaches, cantaloupe, tangerines, rutabagas, pumpkins, and other all orange-skinned fruits and vegetables. For spices and herbs, the following authors' books (see the Bibliography) might also be helpful: Hanna Kroeger, ©1995; Mary Summer Rain, ©1990; Jethro Kloss, ©1995; John Lust, ©1974; and Steven Foster and James A. Duke, ©1990.
Stones	Some of the stones related to the color orange are agate, butlerite, botryogen, carnallite, celstite, crocoite, fourmarierite, grossular garnet, hopeite, jasper, opal, sphalerite, tourmaline, vanadinite. Two books authored by Melody, ©1991 and ©1991 (see the Bibliography), might be helpful, or check for other books at your public library.
Plants (trees, flowers, etc.)	The following authors' books might be helpful (see the Bibliography): Allen J. Coombes, ©1992; Steven Foster and James A. Duke, ©1990; Ellen Evert Hopman, ©1992; Frank D. Venning and Saito C. Manabuo, ©1984. Or check for books at your public library.
Animals	The following authors' books might be helpful (see the Bibliography): Ted Andrews, ©1993; John Bull and John Farrand, Jr., ©1977; Miklos Udvardy, ©1977; and John O. Whitaker, ©1980.
Other	There may be another attribute for you to explore.

Yellow. Solar Plexus Chakra

Attribute	Characteristics associated with the Solar Plexus chakra or the color yellow
Focus	Mental/emotional personal power.
Related colors	Yellow, only. A grayish-yellow color typically signifies fear.
Glands	Spleen.
Musical note	E.
Symbol	Square means "Unity." The square may be used as **protection** over the Solar Plexus chakra. God Aspect. Golden signifies the following soul qualities: Wisdom, Knowledge, Assurance, and Astral mental forces. Symbolizes thought and mental concentration. Light and presence of intellect. Bright, optimistic, intelligent, and capable (business). High-spirited. Other positive vibrations are accomplishment, adjusted, attuned, changeable, channel, coexist, decision, employ, enchantment, engaging, erect, in tune, loving place, slender, turn, sunlight, cheerful, suggestive, Enlightenment and perfection, always towards the new. Personal empowerment.
Metals	Relating to the color of yellow are aluminum, barium, cadmium, calcium, chromium, cobalt, copper, gold, manganese, nickel, titanium, strontium, zinc.
Foods (vegetables, fruit, herbs, spices)	Corn, parsnips, onion, squash, yams, apricots, banana, grapefruit, lemon, mangoes, melons, pineapples, and other yellow-skinned fruits and vegetables. Honey, grains, eggs, cheese, butter, oils. For spices and herbs, the following authors' books (see the Bibliography) might also be helpful: Hanna Kroeger, ©1995; Mary Summer Rain, ©1990; Jethro Kloss, ©1995; John Lust, ©1974; and Steven Foster and James A. Duke, ©1990.
Stones	Some stones related to the color yellow are amber, autenite, beaverrite, beryllonite, beryl, brazilianite, calcite, carnotite, cat's eye, citrine, cookeite, endlichite, goyazite, halite, heliodor, opalized wood, orpiment, etc. Also, two books authored by Melody, ©1991 and ©1991 (see the Bibliography), might be helpful, or check for other books at your public library.
Plants (trees, flowers, etc.)	The following authors' books might be helpful (see the Bibliography): Allen J., ©1992; Steven Foster and James A. Duke, ©1990; Ellen Evert Hopman, ©1992; Frank D. Venning and Saito C. Manabuo, ©1984. Or check for books at your public library.
Animals	The following authors' books might be helpful (see the Bibliography): Ted Andrews, ©1993; John Bull and John Farrand, Jr., ©1977; Miklos Udvardy, ©1977; and John O. Whitaker, ©1980.
Other	There may be another attribute for you to explore.

Green. Heart Chakra

Attribute	Characteristics associated with the Heart chakra or the color green
Focus	Mental and Spiritual Healing, feelings. Attunement.
Related colors	Green, Pink. **Cosmic color green signifies the element of earth and relates to our sense of smell (nose).** Green is the common denominator in all Nature, the color of balanced strength. It is soothing to the Soul at all times. Pale green signifies healing power. Grayish green signifies pessimism, envy.
Glands	Thymus.
Musical note	F.
Symbol	Circle means "Dance of Life." The circle may be used as **protection** over the Heart chakra. Individualism, regeneration healing, honoring nature and all forms of life, energy, and supply. Keynote of Ego. Growth. Tendency towards prosperity and success. Multiplicity of ideas. Animated, versatile, thoughtful, adaptable. Freedom from bondage. Independence, new life. Other positive vibrations relating to the color green and the Heart chakra are abstain, accommodate, attainment, buoyancy, clearing, compassion, determination, Divine, expect, loving, moving, perfect, precise, support, writing, youngster, harmony, perseverance, deep rooted, proud.
Metals	Aluminum, chromium, cobalt, copper, nickel, platinum, sodium, titanium.
Foods (vegetables, fruit, herbs, spices)	Related to the color green: celery, lettuce, all green vegetables and fruits. For spices and herbs, the following authors' books (see the Bibliography) might be helpful: Hanna Kroeger, ©1995; Mary Summer Rain, ©1990; Jethro Kloss, ©1995; John Lust, ©1974; and Steven Foster and James A. Duke, ©1990.
Stones	Some of the stones related to the color green are adamite, agate, ajoite, amazonite, andradite, antlerite, anylite, apophylite, arthurite, aurichalcite, bloodstone, chrysocolla, chrysoprase, clinochlore, conichalcite, cuproadamite, diabantite, dioptase, grossular garnet, kyanite, malachite, nephrite, obsidian, olivenite, sapphire, variscite, woodwardite. Also, two books authored by Melody, ©1991 and ©1991 (see the Bibliography), might be helpful, or check for other books at your public library.
Plants (trees, flowers, etc.)	The following authors' books might be helpful (see the Bibliography): Allen J. Coombes, ©1992; Steven Foster and James A. Duke, ©1990; Ellen Evert Hopman, ©1992; Frank D. Venning and Saito C. Manabuo, ©1984. Or check for books at your public library.
Animals	The following authors' books might be helpful (see the Bibliography): Ted Andrews, ©1993; John Bull and John Farrand, Jr., ©1977; Miklos Udvardy, ©1977; and John O. Whitaker, ©1980.
Other	There may be another attribute for you to explore.

Blue. Throat Chakra

Attribute	Characteristics associated with the Throat chakra or the color blue
Focus	Mental and Spiritual healing, power center, communication, power and creative energy.
Related colors	Sky blue. **Cosmic color blue is the element of ether, relates to the sensation of sound (ears).** Bright blue signifies self-reliance, confidence, loyalty, and sincerity. Poised, calm, spiritually aware. Cool and aloof. Tendency toward teaching, singing, or lecturing. Grayish blue signifies melancholy. Ice blue signifies an intellectual tendency.
Glands	Thyroid, parathyroid.
Musical note	G.
Symbol	Rectangle means "Opportunity." The rectangle may be used as **protection** over the Throat chakra. (A rectangle and word "Opportunity" are also the symbol and its meaning for the Sex chakra.) Heaven's hue. Inspiration. Truth. Color of fortune. An artistic, harmonious nature and spiritual understanding. Other positive vibrations relating to the color blue are willing, abstain, assurance, beautiful, best, change, enjoy, fulfilled, involved, moving, precious, sign, simple, speak out/upturn, self-expression.
Metals	Aluminum, cobalt, cadmium, copper, lead, manganese, nickel, tin, titanium, zinc.
Foods (vegetables, fruit, herbs, spices)	Plums, grapes, and all blue fruits and vegetables related to the color blue. For spices and herbs, the following authors' books (see the Bibliography) might be helpful: Hanna Kroeger, ©1995; Mary Summer Rain, ©1990; Jethro Kloss, ©1995; John Lust, ©1974; and Steven Foster and James A. Duke, ©1990.
Stones	Some of the stones related to the color blue are azurite, ceruleite, chalcanthite, cyanotrichite, kyanite, lapis lazuli, larimar stone, lazurite, obsidian, opal, blue quartz, sapphire, sodalite, tiger eye. Also, two books authored by Melody, ©1991 and ©1991 (see the Bibliography), might be helpful, or check for other books at your public library.
Plants (trees, flowers, etc.)	The following authors' books might be helpful (see the Bibliography): Allen J. Coombes, ©1992; Steven Foster and James A. Duke, ©1990; Ellen Evert Hopman, ©1992; Frank D. Venning and Saito C. Manabuo, ©1984. Or check for books at your public library.
Animals	The following authors' books might be helpful (see the Bibliography): Ted Andrews, ©1993; John Bull and John Farrand, Jr., ©1977; Miklos Udvardy, ©1977; and John O. Whitaker, ©1980.
Other	There may be another attribute for you to explore.

Using the Inner Art of Dowsing in the Search for My Spiritual Enlightenment

Indigo. Brow (Third Eye) Chakra

Attribute	Characteristics associated with the Brow chakra or the color indigo
Focus	Spiritual visualization, cosmic consciousness, intuition, healing. (Also, please review books listed at the beginning of this section, "Aura and Chakra Colors, Chakras and Their Meanings for Healing," or check your public library.)
Related colors	Indigo.
Gland	Pituitary
Musical note	A.
Symbol	Square means "Unity." The square may be used as **protection** over the brow chakra. (The square and word "Unity" are also the symbol and its meaning for the Solar Plexus chakra.)
	Very high spiritual vibration. High intuition. Ability to meditate deeply. Follow inner guidance in making decisions and finding solutions. Dedication to high ideals. Worshipful sense. Expansion of inner vision and awareness. Intuitive, psychic, seeing.
	The new color of the New Race.
	Other positive vibrations relating to the color indigo and the brow chakra are admiration, aware, buoyancy, comparable, determination, erect, in tune, pride, relief, devotion, serenity, Divine mind.
Metals	Chromium, copper, iron, strontium, titanium.
Foods (vegetables, fruit, herbs, spices)	You may take foods from the colors of blue and violet.
	For spices and herbs, the following authors' books (see the Bibliography) might be helpful: Hanna Kroeger, ©1995; Mary Summer Rain, ©1990; Jethro Kloss, ©1995; John Lust, ©1974; and Steven Foster and James A. Duke, ©1990.
Stones	Some stones related to the color indigo are cordierite, julienite, kyanite, lapis lazuli, lazurite, obsidian, opal, sapphire, sodalite, tiger eye.
	Also, two books authored by Melody, ©1991 and ©1991 (see the Bibliography), might be helpful, or check for other books at your public library.
Plants (trees, flowers, etc.)	The following authors' books might be helpful (see the Bibliography): Allen J. Coombes, ©1992; Steven Foster and James A. Duke, ©1990; Ellen Evert Hopman, ©1992; Frank D. Venning and Saito C. Manabuo, ©1984. Or check for books at your public library.
Animals	The following authors' books might be helpful (see the Bibliography): Ted Andrews, ©1993; John Bull and John Farrand, Jr., ©1977; Miklos Udvardy, ©1977; and John O. Whitaker, ©1980.
Other	There may be another attribute for you to explore.

Violet or Purple. Crown Chakra

Attribute	Characteristics associated with the Crown chakra or the color violet or purple
Focus	Spiritual wisdom, integration, comic consciousness, appreciation, visionary, mystical.
Related colors	Electric ultraviolet, iridescent, mother-of-pearl, rainbow, white. **Cosmic color violet is the element of air, and relates to the sense of touch (skin).** Violet is more the spiritual part, relating to selfless, self-sacrificing service. Purple crowns the higher mind, more the temporal part, more related to the earthly plane, dignity. Orchard color signifies idealism.
Gland	Pineal.
Musical note	B.
Symbol	Circle and Bean, where the circle means "Dance of Life" for Crown chakra, and the Bean (shaped like a lima bean) is the "Beamer toward the Universe/God." This is called the Neo Brain above the Crown chakra. The Circle and Bean may be used as **protection** over the Crown chakra. Extremely high vibration. Appeals to more sensitive and soul-conscious people rather than the masses. Path of service and dedication to higher ideals. Combines spirituality of blue with addition of red elements of vitality and power. Color of the Initiate and Adept. Ray of power and influence. True greatness and worthiness. Non-attached love and wisdom. Other positive vibrations relating to the color purple/violet and the crown chakra are absolute, assurance, At-one-ment, bliss, brand new, correct, encouraged, erect, expecting, involved, perfect.
Metals	Aluminum, barium, calcium, cobalt, iron, manganese, rubidium, strontium, titanium.
Foods (vegetables, fruit, herbs, spices)	Aubergine, purple broccoli, beet-tops, blackberries, purple grapes, etc. For spices and herbs, the following authors' books (see the Bibliography) might be helpful: Hanna Kroeger, ©1995; Mary Summer Rain, ©1990; Jethro Kloss, ©1995; John Lust, ©1974; and Steven Foster and James A. Duke, ©1990.
Stones	Amethyst, ametrine, charoite, damsonite, fluorite, halite, jadeite, kunzite, obsidian, strombolite, tourmaline, quartz. Also, two books authored by Melody, ©1991 and ©1991 (see the Bibliography), might be helpful, or check for other books at your public library.
Plants (trees, flowers, etc.)	The following authors' books might be helpful (see the Bibliography): Allen J. Coombes, ©1992; Steven Foster and James A. Duke, ©1990; Ellen Evert Hopman, ©1992; Frank D. Venning and Saito C. Manabuo, ©1984. Or check for books at your public library.
Animals	The following authors' books might be helpful (see the Bibliography): Ted Andrews, ©1993; John Bull and John Farrand, Jr., ©1977; Miklos Udvardy, ©1977; and John O. Whitaker, ©1980.
Other	There may be another attribute for you to explore.

OTHER COLORS THAT MAY SHOW UP IN OUR AURIC FIELD

There are many more colors that relate to colors of aura/chakras listed in the previous section, and they come from the main colors. They can be light, pale, medium, deep, dark, mix/match, interwoven, blended, etc.

Listed below are additional colors that might be seen in one's aura.

Pink	A mystic color. Quiet, refined, modest. Fond of beauty and artistic surroundings. Great and lasting devotion. Supreme, excellent, perfection.
Brown	Relating directly to our physical body/senses. Also relating to Roots, home and the company of its own kind, family security. Capacity for organization, and orderly management. Industry and diligent work. Ruling color of convention. Starting point of ambition and power. Material and commercial. Painstaking perseverance. Earthy. Dull brown signifies low energy.
Cobalt	The Purity of your Soul.
Gray	Fear, boredom, no-man's-land, walling everything off, uncommitted, uninvolved, concealment, repressed anger.
Black	Depression, extinction, nothingness, renunciation, relinquishment, surrender. It is also a protective color.
White	Highly spiritual (rarely seen), pure.
Gold or Silver	Pure knowing and intuition. Very developed psychically. Excellent, precious, opportunity.
Transparent	Reader, restorer, loved, void, truth, pure light.
Clear	Endurance, here/in the Now, clear decision-maker, uses Divine blueprint, mystic.
Other	There may be another color for you to explore.

POSSIBLE PROBLEMS/ISSUES/UNWANTED INFLUENCES WITH AURAS, CHAKRAS, OR MERIDIANS

Dowse to find out whether it's beneficial at this time to investigate problems/issues/ unwanted influences listed below.

- Malfunctions of magnetic field or electro-biochemical field.
- Balloons, holes, gaps, enlargements of areas on aura.
- Closed.
- Too open.
- Unbalanced, improper energy flow.
- Not enough energy.
- Others. There are more problems/issues/unwanted influences that you may need to name.

RESOLUTION OF PROBLEMS/ISSUES/UNWANTED INFLUENCES WITH AURAS, CHAKRAS, OR MERIDIANS

Dowse to find out whether a resolution below is beneficial at this time.

- Need to balance the auric field because it is overextended or underdeveloped.
- Need to work with the auric field, manipulate, see, heal and seal, focus on.
- Work with one or more of the elements: Earth, Water, Wood, Metal, Air.
- You may choose one of the Healing Methods listed below to balance:

– Belief system	– Affirmation
– Chakra	– Mantra
– Colors	– Meditation
– Energy movement	– Numbers
– Gemstones	– Nature, which includes animals,
– Healers	desert, earth, flowers, herbs, plants,
– Imagination	trees, sand, mountains, etc.
– Visualization	– People
	– Positive thought, Let go, etc.

- Others. There are more resolutions that you may need to explore.

OUR BELIEF SYSTEM/VALUE SYSTEM

We may be blinded by Organized Belief Systems/Value Systems, some of which are listed below:

- Our religion
- Anything adapted from parents, relatives, siblings, teachers, employers, employees, friends, and churches
- Mind control
- Educational and financial institutions
- Relationship (sexual, social, family, etc.)

Any belief system has the potential to positively or negatively affect our entire life if we are not aware of it. It also may lock us in and hinder us on our Path of Enlightenment.

ORGANIZED BELIEF SYSTEMS/VALUE SYSTEMS

Below are listed a number of religions or belief systems, used by humanity, that may influence us. (This list is by no means complete.) Be tolerant of others' searches for their connection to the Divine. Each person or being connects in their own way. We are not all alike.

- Christian-based beliefs
    - Adventist (Seventh Day; Church of God)
    - Baptist (27 groups)
    - Church of Christ Scientist (Christian Science)
    - Church of Jesus Christ of Latter Day Saints (Mormons)
    - Eastern Orthodox
    - Episcopal (Anglican)
    - Friends (Quaker)
    - Greek Orthodox
    - Jehovah's Witness
    - Lutheran
    - Mennonite (similar to Amish)
    - Methodist
    - Mysticism (Christian)
    - Nazarene
    - Orthodox Presbyterian
    - Pentecostal (Assembly of God, Four Square)
    - Roman Catholic
    - Russian Orthodox
    - Universalist
    - Unitarian

    - Satanism (Belief in God, Christ but focuses on evil/opposite of God)

(continued on the next page)

(continued from the previous page)

- Animism

  It is the modern belief in forces of nature, and was the focus of the ancient ("dead") religions: Greek, Etruscan, Sumerian, etc.

- Buddhism
  - Buddhist Churches of America
  - Theravadan Buddhism (Burma, Ceylon)
  - Zen Buddhism (Japanese)
  - Chinese Buddhism
  - Tibetan Buddhism

- Confucianism (Chinese)
- Hinduism (India)

  Thousands of varieties of worship: Yoga, Gods/Goddesses, etc.

- Islam
  - Muslim/Moslem
  - Black Muslim
  - Sufi (Mystical Islam)
- Judaism (Orthodox, Conservative, Reformed, etc.)
- Native American religions
- New Age

  New Age is a term for "modern" spiritual outlook. It incorporates beliefs in multiple areas—auras, chakras, energy vortexes, and powers and properties of plants or minerals, etc. One's practice may include all or only a few aspects. It focuses on recognition of one's own innate abilities with the assistance of other forces.

- Pantheism—the belief that all things within the universe are of the Divine.
- Rastafarianism
- Self-directed (Eclectic)

  Consult encyclopedias and other references for religions and religious materials.

- Shamanism
- Spiritualism

  It may incorporate a variety of religious outlooks with many aspects. It looks at the power of Higher Force and its manifestations in the world around you.

- Taoism (Chinese)
- Shintoism (Japanese)

(continued on the next page)

(continued from the previous page)

- Voodoo

  It is an ancient African-based belief system.

- Wiccan/Paganism

  It focuses on natural forces and a person's ability to make use of them.

PERSONAL BELIEFS

Be aware of words, spoken or written. They influence thought, belief, motivation, etc.

What is language? It's the tongue, human speech, the expression of thoughts by words or articulate sounds; the aggregate of words employed by any community for intercommunication; the speech peculiar to a nation; words appropriate to or especially in any branch of knowledge, whether seen, spoken, heard or written.

After we hear self-talk enough, we believe it. Then it's up to us to get out from this vibration. God gave us Free Will; how do we use our Will? Listed below are examples of self-talk that can become personal belief:

- You are too old.
- You are too young.
- You are sick.
- You do not fit in.
- You are not intelligent.
- You are dumb.
- You do not have enough.
- You need to move.
- You are poor.
- You are too rich.
- You do not have the right contacts.
- You are not good enough.
- Others. There are more examples of self-talk you may like to be aware of.

WHETHER TO KEEP OR DELETE A BELIEF

What you feel you need, you keep. What you don't need, you delete.

PROBLEMS OR ISSUES RELATED TO RELIGIONS/BELIEF SYSTEMS

Dowse to find out whether it's beneficial at this time to investigate a problem or issue listed below.

- Belief system is too limiting, structured, rigid.
- Belief system gives inadequate support.
- Belief system lacks structure.
- Others. There are more issues or problems you may like to search for.

RESOLUTIONS TO CHANGE RELIGIONS/BELIEF SYSTEMS

Dowse to find out whether it's beneficial at this time to investigate an action or comment listed below in order to resolve an issue with a religion/belief system.

- Need to:
  - Find a new system.
  - Stay with an existing belief system.
  - Work within religious system to develop self.
  - Focus on working with others' self development.
- Become: missionary, teacher, lay person, disciple, volunteer.
- Belief/religious system is harmful/is helpful.
- Need to devote more/less: time, effort, money.
- Create books, poetry, music, artwork, dances, rituals.
- Sing hymns.
- Meditate
- Others. There are more resolutions you may like to explore.

- Religion/belief system: conscious, subconscious.
- Find belief system that:
  - Focuses on social interaction.
  - Focuses on personal development.
  - Balances social/individual aspects.
- Should consider: becoming part of clergy, leaving clergy.
- Rely on own intuition in regards to beliefs.
- Read more/read less religious material.
- Problems with fellow members, religious hierarchy, clergy.
- Pray.
- Preach.

PLEASE DO NOT JUDGE OTHERS' BELIEFS

As we look to Heaven and ask for guidance, we acknowledge the Truth—that we believe in a Higher Source. Some call it God, Jehovah, Buddhist Dharma, Yahweh, Jesus, Allah, Mother Mary, the Tao, etc. In Truth it is all the same; it is the Vibration we are able to relate to.

The Church we attend, the people we are able to relate to—that is our Truth at that time.

As a human being, we must be very careful of judging another for their belief system. There are many religions in this world, and whatever they believe is their Truth. Please do not judge another person, for you are judging yourself.

The following passage from the Bible is talking about Unconditional Love:

Thou shalt love thy neighbour as thyself.
There is none other commandment greater than these.

St. Mark 12:31

What does that mean to you? Does it refer only to your neighbor next door? No, not at all. It means your neighbor across the country, across the sea, across the world, no matter the culture or religion to which they belong.

Please honor, respect and love unconditionally each individual for being in their own Truth.

KARMA AND ITS INFLUENCES

Also see "Soul Levels" under "Soul Influences."

As above, so below.

Whatever ye sow, so shall ye reap.

For every action, there is a reaction.

Voids must be filled.

All things change.

Give to receive.

Polarities seek balance.

In Sanskrit, karma means "reaction follows action," that is, what you send out, you get back. Karma is neither good nor bad. It may be painful, but it promotes growth. From lifetime to lifetime, man determines his destiny by his action, including thoughts, feelings, words and deeds.

Ego attachments are a source of karma or are apt to create it. One needs to develop an attitude of detachment. (This does not mean non-caring. One may actually care more deeply and risk more when detached. Also, see "Divine Principles of Truth," Principle #12.)

The concept "eye for an eye" does not help let go karma. Rather, the concept and use of forgiveness helps let go karma. One might also let go karma by complete awareness of what one does, feels or thinks. It is also helpful to ask a Higher Force to help you with letting go. Or, make a short list of your offenses against others, and vice versa, that you need to give up; then decide which is most important to you to let go, and then go to work on letting go.

After letting go Karma, one must change or else attract the same or similar situation again, often worse than before. In order to grow, we must undergo learning experiences.

Our attitudes and feelings toward lessons and experiences make the difference in how we travel through our lives. Often an experience is not the result of karma but is an opportunity being presented to us. We must be aware that new energies are encountered during our growth or evolution as spiritual beings.

Often, opportunities give one the sense of being pushed towards a situation, while a karmic situation often gives the sense of being pulled toward the action.

KINDS OF KARMA

Personal Karma

Personal karma is either situational or attitudinal.

- **Situational karma.** Anything you have done to someone else in a past life is returned in kind to you by that person in this life. (This cycle goes on for several lifetimes.)
- **Attitudinal karma.** For example, all past life anger toward life or toward others affects all you do in this life (This karma causes one to attract attitudes and feelings similar to what you send out). Be aware of unhealthy attitudes, and let them go. For example, it is best to fill yourself with Love.

Karma of Others

People often get caught up in other people's karma. At times it is good to help and assist others. However, before doing so, use prayer, intuition, and consideration to see if it is in the best interest of all to get involved. You can create karma when your effort to "help" someone actually interferes with their growth process. You thus become entangled and tied to that person through the law of karma.

Worrying or interfering when you shouldn't, is a cause of entanglement. Rather than worry, send blessings.

Group Karma

A group can develop karma that needs to be worked on as individuals or as the group that initiated the karma. Be aware and conscious of your group and its actions; don't create unwanted or unnecessary karma.

Conscious Choice Karma

Prior to coming into this life, a person makes a choice as to what and how much karma they wish to let go or develop to enhance their growth process. For example, some people may choose to develop an illness and then exceed the limitations supposedly placed upon them by that illness. Again, remember that we play a strong role in choosing our lives and what occurs during them.

Karmic Record

This record is said to be written in the book of Life (in Akasha) and in the etheric body. It is a record of an individual's use of energy after the descent of the Soul into matter. It is a record of cause-effect sequences made by the Soul's interaction with other Souls.

POSSIBLE SOURCES OF KARMIC INFLUENCES

1. Creating karma: Law of Cause and Effect and Retribution.

2. Energy in action: unfinished business—in this life, in past life or lives.

3. Karma residue: time karma.

4. Karma associated with empires, civilizations, countries, states, provinces, a city, town, village, or estate. (For clues, check a world history or atlas, and check through time periods.)

5. Karma associated with continents: Asia, Africa, Europe, North America, South America, Australia, Antarctica.

6. Family karma or another's Karma.

7. Group karma or race Karma.

8. Personal karma: situational or attitudinal (see "Personal Karma" on the preceding page).

RESOLUTION OF KARMIC INFLUENCES

Dowse to find out whether a resolution, below, is beneficial at this time.

- Receive, to balance.
- Focus on karma.
- Regression is helpful.
- Read less religious material.
- Others. There are more resolutions you may like to explore.

- Give, to balance.
- Do not focus on karma.
- Regression is not helpful.
- Read more religious material.
- Change an attitude.

WORKING WITH INFLUENTIAL FORCES TOWARDS OUR ENLIGHTENMENT

Often, sensitive people feel a presence or a change in their surroundings. More often than not, all that is needed is a simple request that the being/entity leave and seek the White Light. Many times a presence may also be that of a relative or a loved one that feels as though certain issues have not been resolved or certain life tasks have not been completed.

ASK ABOUT THE PURPOSES AND TYPES OF INFLUENTIAL FORCES (POSSESSIONS, ENTITIES, ATTACHMENTS, AFFLICTIONS, ETC.) INVOLVED

Use your dowsing method to ask, "Is (are) there an influential force(s) involved with me?" Ask, "For each force that's involved with me, what is its purpose—Positive, Negative, Neutral, Beneficial, Harmful, Dangerous?" Ask, "Is (are) the force(se) listed below?"

Column 1	Column 2	Column 3
• Atlantean entities	• Automatic writing	• Black magic entities
• Body bound entities	• Crawl-in (see below)	• Curse put on you or on family from this lifetime or past life time
• Dark forces	• Disembodied Soul entity	• Earthbound entities
• Emotional entities	• Fear entities	• Gargoyles
• Gremlins	• Haunted house	• Hospital (any place you go has vibrations)
• Lemurian entities	• Mass consciousness (a curse from another dimension)	• Mental entities
• Ouija board	• Past life entities	• Poltergeist
• Residue haunting (residual)	• Satanic entities	• Scared Soul entities
• Spell	• Spirit possession of the Soul	• Voodoo spell
• Walk-in (see below)	• Witchcraft spell	• Zombie
	• Lost Soul (see below)	
	• Others. There are more kinds of influential forces that you may need to name.	

Crawl-in. It is a Soul that enters a mother's womb. This Soul has been weakened by past experiences and requires special care. It may be born with karmic ties and physical defects necessary for its growth and development and also for the growth and development of people it encounters.

Walk-in. Some Souls choose to leave the earthly plane. In some cases, when a Soul leaves, another may take its place. The replacement is known as a "walk-in Soul." Often this Soul is intent on helping with world Enlightenment. It can be a different aspect of the same Soul—Soul-family aspect.

Lost Soul. A Soul that became confused and did not know which way to turn to go towards the Light.

Just a few more Vibrations that may be of importance

Dowse to find out whether it's beneficial at this time to investigate the Vibrations below.

- Astral shell
- Alcoholic demon
- Demonic possession
- Drug-related entities
- Taro

- Earth vampire
- Obsession in blood
- Portal, an opening or gate into another dimension or into your being
- Others. There are more kinds of Vibrations that you may need to name.

- Physical leeches
- Parasites
- Reptilian entities
- Robot
- Space entities (relating to spasms)

CAUTIONS ABOUT ATTRACTING UNWANTED FORCES

People full of Light energy attract many dark pockets of influential forces that are searching for Light. People consciously on the Path must have constant awareness and protection to guard for and help these influential forces to move on to the Divine Light (not with malice, but with kind intent and love). If an influential force is not ready to be helped, respect that; later, when the influential force is ready, you can help it.

Thoughts of jealousy, hate, destruction, envy, and fear invite and attract these same feelings which are part of many incarnate and unincarnate beings. It is in one's best interest to avoid and refrain from indulging these emotions, or one risks encounters and attachments.

Drugs, alcohol and other substances harmful to body, mind, spirit and Soul also tend to weaken and leave people open to influential forces.

If you collect artifacts, antiques, stones, or crystals, or if you've stored or have been given a dead animal such as a bird, an insect, or road kill, be aware that these items might be anchoring points for unwanted forces (human and nonhuman).

Be aware of beings (sometimes people) who want to get control of your mind, Soul, or being. They use any means that are at their disposal. Be aware of the use of electronic, chemical, hypnotic, or sexual methods. Often, they may try to reach and/or influence you on the feelings or emotional level. Psychic "hooks" may also be placed upon you. These are used to reel you in, pull on you, distract you, and may often cause a sense of physical pain or discomfort.

Often, your best defenses are awareness and saying a prayer of protection invoking the White Light (see "Surround me with White Light, Golden Light" on page 54). Read about other antidotes on pages that follow.

POSSIBLE EFFECTS OR AFFLICTIONS RESULTING FROM UNWANTED FORCES

1. Sudden changes in behavior: eating, drinking, or sleeping.

2. Increased negative emotions: depression, increase in anger, rebelliousness, fear, panic, suicidal.

3. Physical pain, with usually no lab or x-ray finding. Pain that does not respond to traditional medical treatment.

4. Serious illness (unknown cause): persistent non-responsive infections, possibly caused by attached earthbound entities who suffered from or died of infection. (When an influential force leaves, the infection leaves.) Also, unusual inflammatory or metabolic disorders and blood dyscrasias.

5. Loss of energy: sudden decrease of physical energy.

6. Sudden onset of alcohol or drug abuse: a possessing entity is usually one who indulged in drugs or alcohol. When the entity leaves, so does the urge for alcohol or drugs.

7. Memory and concentration problems: one who is accustomed to easy learning and high grades abruptly changes to low performance and poor grades.

8. Inner voices: voices that express a reaction or point of view that differs from one's normal perspective.

9. Multiple personality disorder: multiples are often caused by entities. Careful evaluation is necessary.

10. Repetitious nightmares: a dream contains elements of violence or of struggle against threatening forces.

GUIDELINES: WHAT TO DO BEFORE WORKING WITH INFLUENTIAL FORCES

Remember the following guidelines before you leap into working with yourself or another person or with influential forces.

Examine Your Relationships

Remember that living beings can also create possessive forces

As we live daily lives in our societies, we come across all fashions and sorts of people. I have discovered over the years that it is best to be quite choosy about whom you let into your life. As you open your heart and life to people, be aware the type of people you are letting in. People wear facades, ornaments and entrapments, often representing themselves in a way that hides their true motives. Please also understand that people may not even be aware of motives under which they function. So regard each person as another Soul on its journey trying to discover the truth of itself and life.

Many people cope in existence by living off others. No, I do not just mean living off others' wealth. It could be living off their emotional energy, sexual energy, intelligence, creativity, a whole multitude of things.

Do you feel odd or drained after you have been with this person? As these people live in your life—be they spouse, friend, lover, boss—you need an awareness of how they respect you and how you respect yourself in that relationship. You can choose to give away, unaware, your energy to these people.

Key words to be aware of in a relationship

Dowse to find out whether it's beneficial at this time to investigate a keyword below.

- Zapped
- Confused
- Questioning of self
- Uncertain
- Drugged
- Others. There are more keywords that you may need to list.

Protect Oneself with Prayer

Be aware that all thoughts and feelings are not necessarily your own. Use your dowsing method to learn which prayers below are most effective for you at this time.

God Force is within me and surrounds me.

Nothing can hinder or harm me.

SURROUND ME WITH WHITE LIGHT, GOLDEN LIGHT

Please Dear Lord,
Put your pure White Light of Protection and Golden Light of
Unconditional Love in me, around me, and through me,
so only positive thoughts enter my mind and
positive thoughts come from my mind.

Whatever negativity comes from me or towards me,
please let it go instead to you for healing. Thank you.

Amen.

WHAT I NEED IN ORDER TO ACT

I do not have to have all the answers.

I do not need to see all answers or have all the solutions before I act.

I need to take heart and fill myself with thoughts of love,
courage, and Highest Vision.
I need only to aim for the good of all.

The Lord shall preserve your going out and your coming in from
this time forth, and even for evermore.

Psalm 121:8

I am here only to be truly helpful.

I am here to represent him who sent me.
I do not have to worry about what to say or what to do,
Because he who sent me, directs me.
I am constant to be wherever he wishes,
Knowing he goes there with me.

I am healed as I let him teach me to help others heal themselves.

Author Unknown. (Thank you and blessings to you.)

Even though I walk through the valley of the shadow of death,
I fear no evil for thou art with me. Thy rod and thy staff they comfort me.

Psalm 23:4

LIVING IN GOD'S VIBRATION

"I am meek in heart." I have no fear as to what men and other beings think or say concerning me, for I do all things for and in the Lord's Vibration. I leave the results with him. I am not bound in personal consciousness.

The joy of the Lord is my strength, and I am positive, healthy, happy, and fearless and am free to live in God's harmonious Vibration. Love is always active in my heart and mind. I am thankful for total wholeness in my being. Amen

Protect Oneself with Remedies

A few remedies are listed below.

- Take a bath, add bath salts, and/or enjoy aromatherapy.
- Burn Sage in and all around the house, and waft the smoke over yourself. Or burn incense.
- Wear silk.
- Wear cobalt blue-colored clothing, or imagine the color surrounding you.
- Wear cobalt blue-colored jewelry, or any kind of jewelry or symbol that provides to the wearer a feeling or meaning of protection, like a Cross, yen/yin sign, etc.
- Hang a Cross in the room, or wear a Cross as a necklace. The horizontal bar of the Cross symbolizes keeping in balance on the earthly plane. The vertical bar symbolizes your connection with the Source/God.
- Cleaning, clearing, cleansing these Vibrations by lighting candles or by doing conscious clearing of home or living space, work space, etc.

Always Ask for Permission, the Key

Always ask three questions, described below, before you begin any session that might be an unwanted intrusion or that might change your or another a person's attitudes, relationships or any part of their circumstances.

May I/we?	Do I (the dowser) have, at this time, permission on all levels of consciousness of my being to help lift the energies to a Higher place of learning or Light? Do I have, at this time, permission on all levels of consciousness of the person (or animal or other being) that I am working with?
	If I don't get permission from myself and/or from the other being(s), we might go against the Divine Principles of Truth that guide us toward an honest, spiritual, introspective life.
Can I/we?	Do I/we have the ability to do this successfully in this area?
Should I/we?	Is it for the Highest good of all concerned? Is this an appropriate place/environment in which to dowse? Is this an appropriate time to dowse?

REMOVING UNWANTED FORCES

After obtaining permission (described on the previous page), you may want to balance the lower vibration that is causing a person distress.

Beginning the Balance

The following is a question we may need to ask: are we working with the influential force in the human being, or are we working with the human being?

We can say to the influential force, "I feel honored that you came to me and asked to be shown the way to the Light."

Put the Golden Light of Transformation around you, when you working with someone, if you desire to feel the energy, so it gets transmuted into the Light.

Always stay in your own Love, Truth Vibration. When we lower our vibration/frequency we are allowing the lower Frequencies to come into or on us. We always need to have Love in our heart and Soul. Always use prayers of protection, described below.

When we do a Regression, it is very important to clear the lower vibration, otherwise this energy also can get regressed and can cause you harm.

Here is one method: 1) say one of the prayers listed below in *Resolutions and Prayers to Remove Influential Forces*. 2) Use your dowsing method to find out whether the vibration has been balanced 100%, meaning 100% removed and sent to the Light. 3) If the vibration is not balanced 100%, ask more questions and repeat the effort to balance 100%.

&—&—&—&—&—&—&

Ask, and it is given; seek, and you find; knock, and it is opened to you.

For every one who asks receives, and he who seeks finds, and to him who knocks it is opened.

St. Matthew 7:7–8

Resolutions and Prayers to Remove Influential Forces

&—&—&—&—&—&—&

CLEAR THIS ETERNAL BEING OF ALL INFLUENTIAL FORCES

Dear Lord/Father God,
Please bless this eternal being so that it is cleared, on all levels of its being (physical, mental, emotional, spiritual, Soul), of all possessive forces, entities, attachments, afflictions, ghost, spells, curses, etc. I ask that before they leave, they heal the aura of attachment, and I ask they get guided to the Light and surrounded by Unconditional Love. I let you go, you are free.

Bless Love and Light, Bless Love and Light, Bless Love and Light.
Amen.
Thank you dear God/Father. Thy Will be done.

&—&—&—&—&—&—&

FOR THOSE INFLUENTIAL FORCES LOST AND WANDERING

For all those who are lost and wandering, I/we ask that they receive guidance to the Light.

Are you ready to go to the Light? (*If the answer is "No," you may say a short prayer to help them to move on.*)

Thank you dear God/Father.

&—&—&—&—&—&—&

This message came through Anneliese for a client who was living in a room where someone had been murdered, and the ghost of the murdered person was still present. In the message, "me" and "I" refer to that client.

LIFT THIS GHOST TO A HIGHER SCHOOL OF LEARNING

With the permission of God, my permission and the permission of the ghost's Higher Soul Self, I am asking that the Soul of the Ghost be lifted to a Higher school of learning. By the Divine Principles of Truth, this is done.

Bless Love and Light, Bless Love and Light, Bless Love and Light.
Thank you dear God/Father. Amen

Neutralize the Voodoo/Witchcraft Curse or Spell

Dear Lord/Father

I am asking for the Voodoo/Witchcraft curse or spell, past, present, future, to be lifted from all levels of my/our being.

I ask that the Voodoo/Witchcraft curse or spell etc. be neutralized and enhanced into Unconditional Love for the person/being/dimensions that projected the Voodoo/Witchcraft etc. to me/us.

You (the person/being/dimensions that projected) are now free to live in harmony.

I ask that the Divine Source heal the Aura of my/our being.

Bless Love and Light, Bless Love and Light, Bless Love and Light.
Thank you dear Lord/Father

Please bless this house, so it is clean of influential forces.

I ask they receive guidance to the Light.
I let you go, bless you. May your spirit be at peace.
Thank you, God/Father.

This is a request to leave.

If you are not or not of the White or Golden Light, please leave.

Bless Love and Bless Light to you.

My agreement with you is over. Now move to the Light.

Please bless this house

So it is clean of entities and thoughts vibrations of others.

I ask they receive guidance to the pure Light of Love.

I let you go, you are free to roam in the Light of Divinity forever.

Amen. Thank you, Father/Mother/God.

PSYCHIC SENSES AND OTHER RESOURCES

The realization of psychic or extrasensory abilities is not something that is necessarily magical or mystical. Rather, one might consider these as some of the unused abilities that are part of every normal human. They are merely awaiting discovery and use.

In many ways we are only partly alive and aware. We have developed certain patterns of perceiving, thinking and imagining. While these are highly functional, they tend to limit our more expansive abilities, visions and thoughts. Just as we limit our muscles and flexibility by becoming rigid and armored in our movement, we limit our mental powers by covering them with fears, intellectual conflicts and contradictory belief systems.

PSYCHIC SENSES

Psychic healing is the best and highest form of healing known to man. However, even psychic healing cannot effect a permanent cure unless a client changes habits of living and lives in accordance with the Divine Principles of Truth.

Listed below are a number of abilities noted in people throughout human existence. These may also be referred to as extrasensory perception or intuition. Read with an open mind and begin to recognize these as yours.

Psychic Sense	Description
Automatic writing	Writing with the aid of a spiritual guide or teacher. Often one is not conscious of what is being written.
Channeling	Ability to receive direction or information from the Higher Self and universe. Information comes from a source other than the Ego.
Clairaudience	Ability to hear a spirit within or outside one's mind.
Clairsentience	Ability to send and receive thoughts between spirit and self (comparable to telepathy, inner voice in mind).
Clairvoyance	Ability to perceive situations and information at a distance directly, without the mediation of another mind or vehicle.
Precognition	Future access. The ability to perceive information across time and into the future.
Psychokinesis/ Telekinesis	Ability to influence the nature of physical matter without any physical contact, purely with the power of the mind.
Psychometry	Ability to touch something and sense its relation to people, time, etc., entirely through contact with the object. It involves sensing an object's energy field and imprints left upon it.
Retrocognition	Past access. The ability to perceive previous events and information back through time.
Telepathy	Ability to communicate with another mind without the use of any of the basic five senses.
Vibration empathy	The ability to accomplish such sensory activities as divining, reading auras, astral traveling, healing and locating lost objects.

TOOLS, TEACHERS, RESOURCES AND ABILITIES

Using your dowsing method, ask, "Does the table below list at least one tool, teacher, resource or ability that can benefit me now in my search for Spiritual Enlightenment?"

Column 1	Column 2	Column 3
• Ancient art, belief, abilities	• Animal totems	• Aromatherapy
• Astrology	• Crystals	• Dowsing/divining
• Drumming	• Fetishes	• Guru or other teacher
• Healing: psychic, spiritual	• Herbs	• Medicine man/woman
• Numerology	• Out of body (astral projection)	• Palmistry
• Past life regression	• Phrenology	• Psychic surgery
• Quantum physics	• Quest (women)	• Ritual tools
• Rituals or other ceremonies	• Seeing or scrying	• Shaman
• Smoking, smudging, incense	• Subtle body awareness	• Sweat lodge
• Symbology	• Talisman	• Tarot or other card reading
• Trance work	• UFOs	• Vision Quest (men)
	• Others. There are more that you may need to name.	

DESCRIPTIONS OF GUIDES AND GUARDIANS

Many mediums (psychics) state that we are always surrounded by many spiritual beings of whom we are not aware. We have little or no awareness of many levels and planes. Often, we only need to ask for assistance or guidance, and it is provided in one form or another. What is best for our growth and development might not necessarily be something that we enjoy; rather, it might be painful and uncomfortable. We must be open to all our experiences, thereby finding what we are meant to see or develop with this lesson.

Using your dowsing method, ask, "Does the table below list at least one kind of guide or guardian that can benefit me now in my search for Spiritual Enlightenment?"

Kinds of Guides and Guardians

Spiritual guide	This is often a guardian that works with your prior to your coming to the earthly plane. Their purpose is usually karma-influenced, and it can be twofold: • Clear karma owned to you • See that you fulfill your chosen path The guardian is usually opposite in gender, for they can add the love and strength needed. They know what they need to do and work hard to see completion. Trusting in and knowing more of them may help one through this life's journey.
Provider	This guide is assigned to work with you, to bring what you need and give direction. They often work weeks ahead of you. The main work occurs when one strays off the path. They then need to provide a way back to your path. Faith and trust are the best ways to receive assistance from these guides. They usually choose to help the person.
Personal guide	This guide is usually a family member, friend or teacher who wishes to help from the spirit world.
Angels, members of the Brotherhood of Light, etc.	Many religions and belief systems throughout the world have mentioned Angels and gods. Often these are higher evolved beings that are involved in the evolutionary growth process of all beings. They often assist, observe or instruct.

DESCRIPTIONS OF ANGELS (HIGHER BEINGS)

What are Angels? In the Christian Bible, Angels are messengers of God; most often, they portray superhuman traits and sometimes perform miracles. Angels sang a hymn beginning with the words *Gloria in excelsis Deo* announcing the Birth of Jesus: "Glory to God in the Highest, and on Earth peace, good will towards men." (*St. Luke 2:14, the Authorized (King James) Version of the Bible*)

In addition to the information here, books from your public library or a chart about Angels by author Dolfyn, ©1993 (see the Bibliography) might be useful.

YOU NEED ONLY ASK FOR ANGELS' GUIDANCE

Angels are Beings in **Light form**, pure Light Vibration, also in **Human form**, that are guided by me, to help, protect, seal, reveal and perform extraordinary duties.

They are my Divine Messengers of Hope and Understanding.

All you need to do is ask them to be a part in your life. Everything is simple. I have many Angels in my employment, with many specific duties.

Descriptions of Angels

Angel Gabriel. The name used to designate the heavenly messenger, said to explain to Daniel the visions he saw (*Daniel 8:16; 9:21–22, Authorized (King James) Version of the Bible*). In the New Testament he announced the Birth of Jesus and Birth of John the Baptist (*St. Luke 1:26–38*). Angel Gabriel is, in the Jewish and Christian traditions, one of the seven Archangels whose duty is to be the Messenger of Truth.

ANGEL GABRIEL'S MESSAGE

I am the Angel of comfort, sympathy, good tidings, motivation, inspiration, sharing, loyalty, and myth.

I am the Angel of Intuition, of Immediate apprehension or cognition, of Innate or instinctive Knowledge = insight.

I do know without reasoning. Come, invite me into your life.

Angel Gabriel

Angel Michael. The Messenger of God who came to David and said:

> But I will tell you what is inscribed in the Book of Truth: there is none
> who upholds me against these, except Michael your prince.
>
> *Daniel 10:21*

Angel of Light

MESSAGE FROM ANGEL OF LIGHT

As the Angel of Messages and Light, I pray to you to understand me. Sometimes the message might not be clear to you for I do sometimes come in the dream time or through symbols.

Be not afraid for I have much to present to you. I only share and give to you that which you willingly accept. I would never hurt you intentionally for I am God's Divine Being.

> *Angel of Light*

CONNECTING WITH ANGEL VIBRATIONS

Every time I drive, fly or walk, I ask Angel Vibrations to be with me/us and protect me/us. I do not have specific ones. I know God Harold sends the right ones with me at all times. Just trust. (See "Harold Is My Name" under "Relating to God.")

I am mentioning a few Angels and their duties, and it is up to you to search for more, if you truly like and need to work with this vibration.

There are many books about Angels on the market. Search and you will find.

Because my maiden name is Gabriel, I'd like to share this experience with you. During my father's dying process, actually two weeks before his death in 1992, I saw him as an Angel; he was dressed in a white cotton robe, like a light, pure Angel, flowing through the living room in his home where I was staying. My father, the Angel, gave me this message:

> "Say good by, it is time for me to leave this planet Earth and I have
> inspirational work to do some place else."

My father the Angel looked good, felt good and was at peace with his journey.

MESSAGE FROM ANGELS OF LIGHT AND PURITY

Three Angels, pure Beings of Light, surround you.

Embrace these Vibrations for they give you sight.

They lift your Soul in delight,

They refresh your spirit and keep you alive.

Amen

MOTHER'S PRAYER WRITTEN IN MY POETRY BOOK

This is a prayer my mother wrote in my poetry book when I was 14 years old.

Ein Engel Gottes leite Dich auf allen Deinen Wegen,
Gott gebe Dir ein reines Herz als seinen besten Segen.

Deine Mutti,
Braunschweig, September 1st 1950

It means: "An Angel of God leads you on all your ways,
God give you a pure Heart as his best Blessing."

Soul Influences

Perfection of the Soul is through Enlightenment. The Soul remembers what we are at every given moment of life.

PERFECTION OF OUR SOUL

P–	Perfect	S–	Soul
E–	Enlightenment	O–	Oneness
R–	Reaches	U–	Uses
F–	Further	L–	Love
E–	Evolution		
C–	Containing		
T–	Treasures		
I–	In		
O–	Oneness		
N–	Naturally		

Each Soul has chosen, or has been chosen, to enter this life to complete a lesson for growth in the completion of this earthly cycle. There are many levels above and below this earthly cycle.

Each level requires the Soul reach a certain attainment of knowledge and wisdom before it may go on to the next. There are many levels for evolution of the Soul. Souls may also advance levels in a single lifetime. There are also different types of Souls, each with different characteristics, goals and emphases throughout their lifetime.

To explore this aspect further, read a book by author Chelsea Yarbro, ©1979 *Messages from Michael.*

There are many levels of soul development. We need to respect each level of accomplishment. Each Soul has to strive to reach each purpose on each level.

Using the Inner Art of Dowsing in the Search for My Spiritual Enlightenment

Each level has its challenges/opportunities for growth. (See "Soul Levels," below.)

We move forward as fast and as far as we can. The doors are open for each establishment. Move on, be bright and see the new sight and Light, the new level of growth. It takes courage, it takes faith, trust and truth.

Move on my children, be true to yourself.

I am here to guide you at any level you are on. I leave the door open for you to come in, at any time, at any rate, at any speed.

I am here to greet and receive you.

Do not be late.

Amen

Each soul dimension has a different frequency, where we can tap into and communicate, sharing energies on a different level of existence.

Ages of Consciousness

This concerns development of Souls throughout Earth's history. The majority of Souls go through stages mentioned below for "Soul Levels." At present we are at the verge of reaching a majority of Mature and Old Souls in the earth cycle. To encourage soul development, be conscious of incorporating Divine Principles of Truth in your life. (See "Divine Principles of Truth" elsewhere in this book.)

Soul Levels

Before asking about and dowsing for soul levels, ask for permission (described in "Always Ask for Permission, the Key," page 56) on all levels of self and client's consciousness.

When dealing with other people it may be worthwhile to check on the soul level that any particular person is working from. If you are dealing with a person whose soul level is an Infant or Baby Soul, and at times a Young Soul, you may find it difficult to communicate or convince the person of certain points of view. At this time it is not worth your while to become frustrated or upset with these beings.

<u>Accept</u>, <u>honor</u>, <u>respect</u> and <u>bless</u> <u>them</u> for their current stage of growth.

A person becomes stuck on a certain soul level because they have not completed certain <u>Lessons of letting go and accepting</u>, and consequently remain stuck in their present life.

Again, ultimately the person chooses when to grow. There can be no forced growth or change from the outside.

Soul Level before a Human Incarnates on the Earth—Plants, Animals, Mineral Kingdom

- **Unborn Soul**. One who is waiting to incarnate into earthly life. A fragment that has little sense of self-awareness. May yet be closely tied to Divine Energy, or has been separated for a great length of time. Very little influence on others. Many are waiting to rejoin soul groups.

Earthly Soul Levels (when a Human Incarnates on the Earth)

- **Infant Soul**. (Firstborn) Born to simple surroundings. Fearful of new experiences. Does not know difference between right and wrong.
- **Baby Soul**. Focuses preservation of status quo. Highly conservative.
- **Young Soul**. Sets impossible goals (idealistic, materialistic). High sense of Ego. Wants success, acceptance.
- **Mature Soul**. Seeker of higher knowledge. Open to psychic experiences and abilities. An Old Soul is emerging.
- **Old Soul**. Not materialistic. Tends to focus on the service of others. Tends towards individualism, but not forceful as with younger Souls.

Beyond the Earthly Soul Levels

- **Transcendental Soul**. Very high Soul. Incarnates for specific purpose. Prepares way for the "Infinite Soul." Development beyond earthly soul cycles.
- **Infinite Soul**. Comes to Earth to change mankind's course. In touch or harmony with Divine Consciousness.

Eternal Souls (Souls Forever Living in Eternity)

Beyond all the preceding soul levels, we encountered many more Higher Soul Vibrations/Frequencies/Essences. We like to call them ***Eternal Souls***.

SOURCES OF AND RESOLUTIONS FOR SOUL PROBLEMS

> You can't save another Soul, if you are going to lose your own in the process.

For what profit is it to a man if he gains the whole world, and loses his own soul? Or what will a man give in exchange for his soul?

St. Matthew 16:26

Use your dowsing method to learn whether any of the issues listed below affect you at this time.

- Soul fragmentation: disruption of the Soul due to trauma, violation, shock, etc.
- Parts of the Soul have dispersed and need to be retrieved and joined back to the whole
- Is there a veil over the Soul?
- Is the Soul blocked, depleted, subdued, chained, discarded, trapped, split?
- Is a supernatural force in there?
- Some Souls are and feel off-zapped, knotted, tortured, outspoken, escaping, squashed, snipped, beggars, shattered, knotted, rebellious, entangled, living in a pattern, bounded with other, duality habit.
- Other. There are more issues you may like to be aware of at this time.

If one of the issues affects you, use your dowsing method to learn whether any of the resolutions listed below can remove the issue.

- Is the Soul a mate, seeker, twin flame, walk-in, soul master, etc.?
- The Soul needs to be elevated to a higher consciousness.
- The Soul needs cleansing, needs to be heard, needs to be freed.
- The Soul is <u>lost</u>. Seek guidance and help from higher sources to enable the Soul to find the Light.
- Pray, "**Bless Light, Bless Love.**"
- Other. There are more resolutions you may like to be aware of at this time.

Sometimes it feels like we are living in a bird house (nest), very confined, afraid to fly. We are waiting and waiting for something. What is the something we are waiting for, the something that allows us to wake up and truly live in the essence of our Soul? Often an event—an accident, death, sickness or other circumstance—wakes us up, and pushes us out of the nest.

I guess we are waiting for a call from God.

Why are we so afraid to fly?

We feel we need to be protected, so the outside World won't harm us. What is harming us in truth is the Inside world we live in, all the energies we are harboring from long ago, like anger, hurt and pain, judgment, misunderstandings, etc. Those energies give us physical dis-eases, spiritual emptiness, mental disconnection, etc. Is this what we call happiness?

Are you ready to balance your inside world?

Allow God (Holy Spirit) to come into your Life, and you are able to fly free
and live in God's unlimited Energies forever.
You are then ready to embrace all the opportunities coming your way.

There is no more emptiness, only Unconditional Love in your Heart.

How beautiful it feels. Let go, and go with me, my Child.

WISE AND WISER

A wise man learns from experience. A wiser man learns from the experience of others.

Seek and find the Mind of the Divine.

POSITIVE LIFE PATTERN CHANGES THAT MAY ENHANCE YOUR SPIRITUAL ENLIGHTENMENT

You may use your intuition to ascertain which of the following kinds of changes is most important for you at this time in the discovery of your path to Spiritual Enlightenment. Each is described in more detail on pages that follow.

- Body or physical changes to make
- Emotional, intellectual, and mental changes
- Spiritual changes

BODILY OR PHYSICAL CHANGES

Nutritional approaches to daily living

Dowse to find out whether it's useful at this time to investigate an approach listed below. Is the approach beneficial or harmful? If it's beneficial, you might ask, "Is it for my above Highest Good to embrace at this time in my life?"

- Changing your eating habits to balance energies
- Proper food combination
- Vegetarian approach
- Macrobiotic approach
- Blood-type approach
- Pyramid approach
- Fasting
- Eating one/two/three or more meals a day
- Foods that are organically grown, for example, grains, vegetables, fruits, mammal meats, nut meats, seafood, eggs, dairy products, oils, spices, herbs, condiments, sweets, snacks
- Taking nutritional supplements, like vitamins, minerals, enzymes, amino acids, antioxidants, natural food supplements, etc.
- Drinking more liquids like coffee, teas, water, alcohol, beverages, juices
- Focus on relative amount of Proteins, Carbohydrates, etc.
- Others. There are many more approaches you may like to search for.

Nurturing approaches to daily living

Dowse to find out whether it's useful at this time to investigate an approach listed below. Is the approach beneficial or harmful?

- Music, sounds, colors, deep breathing, rest, exercise
- Living on Spiritual Vibration like Prana, Chi, God Force, Light Vibration
- Using New Earth elements (rocks, plants, animals, earth, stars, sun, moon, people, etc.)
- Others. There are many more approaches you may like to search for.

What body systems are affected?

If I was to use one of the approaches above, what part of my being is positively or negatively affected? For an answer, use your intuition to check the systems listed below. (The list is taken from "Step 6: How is the issue manifested on/in/around the body" on page 26 in a book by Anneliese Hagemann and Doris Hagemann, ©1999 *To Our Health.*)

1. Basic Cell System	6. Digestive System	11. Immune System
2. Central and Peripheral Nervous System	7. Reproductive System	12. Chakras/Meridian
3. Sensory Organs	8. Urinary Tract System	13. Subtle Body layers
4. Glands	9. Structural System	14. Other Body Components
5. Circulatory System	10. Respiratory System	

Also, please check for "Conventional and Holistic Healing Methods" on pages 19-21 in our book *To Our Health*.

EMOTIONAL, INTELLECTUAL, AND MENTAL CHANGES

The mind is the generator of thoughts. Thoughts are things; they can do good or harm.

DESIRE DETERMINES DESTINY

You are what your deep, driving desire is.

As your desire is, so is your Will.

As your Will is, so is your deed.

As your deed is, so is your destiny.

Brahadaranyaka Unpanishad

I can not stress enough that your thoughts, speech, and written communications, the vocabulary you use—I mean **"Words"** (**Words are Vibration**)—directly affect you and those around you.

As soon as you think a positive word (higher vibration) or a negative word (low vibration), it is sent out into the Universe and set into action. What you send out, you receive, and you can not cancel it.

In the book *To Our Health*, we list positive and negative vibrations you can check to investigate what words influence your own creation of reality. We recommend, when you dowse, that if you find that you are standing in some of the lower vibrations, it is best to let them go from your total being and then embrace new, positive vibrations into your total being. The results are amazing.

&—&—&—&—&—&—&

Daily I use the affirmations listed below. They may help balance and enhance your being to a state of bliss and Enlightenment.

ANNELIESE'S DAILY AFFIRMATIONS

I am happy.

I am healthy.

I live in harmony.

I am ageless.

I am timeless.

I am a Divine Being.

I am forever young.

I am forever Light.

Let's take a quick look at emotions before we move on.

We have been taught that emotions are a sign of weakness. How very far from the Truth. Emotions reflect the depth and height of human existence. We are here to experience these things. Emotions are expressions of who you are, your mood, your perception, and your state of being. DO NOT BOTTLE UP EMOTIONS. Emotions are meant to be experienced. If you bottle them up, they become harmful to your being. Learn to recognize the vibrations of your emotions. They are good barometers of what is going on inside of you as you experience life. Feel the emotion and gentle joy of connecting with the Divine Source through the flight of a butterfly as it lands on a flower.

Look into our book *To Our Health*, described in the Bibliography, for more information on the emotional and mental aspect of your being.

SPIRITUAL CHANGES

We lost our grasp of/path to God, reaching the lowest point in our Soul's growth, before we could find our stepping stones of "Remembrance." However, we knew they were there.

While discovering our path of Spiritual Enlightenment, the steps we take are totally accepted, acknowledged, desired and granted by the Holy Presence within. We are Celestial Beings (Divine within), making a Vow, Solemn Oath (pledge, promise) to be on track with the Vibration of the Divine. (Also see our comments on the subject of Spirituality under "Why Do We Yearn for Spiritual Enlightenment?")

We remember what we learned, recognize benefits of what has been before, honor and respect it and now move forward on our Enlightenment journey. Recognize your past learning as part of your foundation of Enlightenment. That Knowledge we have and now use to help mankind beyond conception of the norm.

In the journey to discovering self and mission, read and use the workbook *Life's Path— Soul Mission* (see the Bibliography) created with Love by Anneliese. If there is anything you need to balance to reach Spiritual Enlightenment, do it. Balance all the unfinished business and outdated energies, then move ahead on your path of Spiritual Enlightenment.

LIFE EXPERIENCES: EDUCATION, FAMILY, FINANCE, RELATIONSHIP, SEXUAL, SOCIAL, ETC.

Looking back on our life here now on Earth, and perhaps looking back on other lives by applying past life regression or progression, we see, feel and know that experience has led us to where we stand right now in our life.

Life's experiences teach us many lessons; some are painful, others glorious. We need to stay alert to what life has to share with us each day, each moment. What we regard as a curse as we move through it, may in reality be one of the biggest gifts that GOD has ever sent. Again be alert, yes, go through emotions, etc. But remember to step back when you are through the troubling time and see what you have learned from it.

Have no regrets. Accept your journey so far as your soul embodiment of growth.

You may choose to write about "*Your Life's Path you have walked so far.*" What has been unsaid in your life? You may be amazed at what you find out about yourself and all the beautiful people you have met and been in contact with in this life and past, who helped you on your path of Spiritual Enlightenment.

Also you received many special "gifts" from God the Divine; actually, you, the Divine Within, chose them. These gifts, which you may have thought were adversities in your life, actually were stepping stones of faith and understanding. As long as you acknowledge this and do not punish yourself with negative thoughts (such as self hate, indifference, abuse, neglect, accursedness, immobility, worthlessness, being knocked down, resigned, unresolved, suffragette, transgressed, troubled, vindicating feelings) you are doing great.

What did you learn so far here on Earth School from and with your family members, relatives, and friends; through education in schools of understanding; in relation to money, work, sexuality and social behavior?

What did these systems teach you, and how are you applying them on your Spiritual Enlightenment Path? What did birth and death teach you? It does not need to be physical birth or death; it can be mental or spiritual. Look at everything on your calendar of growth.

Using the Inner Art of Dowsing in the Search for My Spiritual Enlightenment

Look at Life's Blessings

What does the word "blessings" mean?

The act of one who blesses; a prayer or solemn wish imploring happiness upon another; a benediction; the act of pronouncing a benediction or blessing; that which promotes temporal prosperity and welfare or secures immortal felicity; any good thing falling to one's lot; a mercy.

From the Educational Book of Essential Knowledge (Webster Dictionary)

The Flower of Forever

I am the Flower of Forever,
I blossom all the time.

I have many colors,
I am truly Divine.

I sing many songs
When the wind blows through me.

I am the AM and PM of time,
The past, present and future.

I am the Divine Source.
Please look at me.

The Flower of Forever is you, my child,
Forever blooming, forever growing, forever Divine and at peace.

Amen

THE POWER OF BLESSINGS. WHAT TO BLESS?

When you have problems with what you feel are bad things, bless the good things in your life.

Bless: Unconditional Love, God, Light and Love, Perfect Living, Your Soul, The Higher Self, Beauty, Energy, Life, Death, Awakening, Harmony, I am One, Your Neighbor, The World, the Government, anything you feel good and like to be a part of.

For example, say, "Bless Love" or "Bless my neighbor Alfred" or "Bless the Government of my country."

By doing so, you are a part of helping others on their way of Enlightenment.

Unconditional Love is the greatest power in the Universe.

STATEMENTS OF BLESSINGS

Bless with Universal Love.

Bless all levels of Love, Bless Love on all Levels.

I am present, I come with Blessed Love, and I depart with Blessed Love.

I am at peace with *<insert your personal Statement here>*.

May the Creator of the Divine Principles of Truth bless my daily life.

Bless this person today so he/she is clear of *<insert your personal Statement here>*.

Please bless my body for the next 24 hours (or forever) so it is clear and clean of negative thought forms, psychic, physical, emotional and mental attacks.

AFFIRMATIONS

What does "affirmation" mean?

- An act of affirming or asserting as truth, a statement
- To assert, positively; to tell with confidence, to aver, declare, to confirm
- To make a solemn assertion or declaration

Our thoughts and actions create our own story. What we think and feel in our mind and heart, we produce in our experience and our life. What we give, we receive. As within, so without. Some affirmations are listed below. You may also use some of them as prayers of protection when using your intuition and Divine Tools for Spiritual Enlightenment.

&—&—&—&—&—&—&

LIST OF AFFIRMATIONS (SOME CAN BE USED AS PRAYERS OF PROTECTION)

Don't give up, just keep on giving.

Perfect Love casts out all fears. I am a channel of Divine Love.

Believe that you are healed.

Everything is in Divine order for my above Highest Good!

Everything is taken care of in its Divine time.

I am in harmony with the good in all portions of my life.

I breathe in Divine Power and exhale Unconditional Love.

I now seal and heal my Aura from all outside influences.

The Spirit of God is in me now and forever.

I am happy, I am healthy, and I live in harmony forever.

Divine Essence is within me, nothing can hinder or harm me.

I am loved; I am taken care of; I am peace; I am thankful; I am joy; I am a spiritual being.

My (God's) words are beautiful.

I am receptive to the Love of God.

God is in me.

I am ready to follow God and his/her/its Will. I am reliable for God.

My choices brought me to where I am, and I am responsible for
my life; no one else is.

Using the Inner Art of Dowsing in the Search for My Spiritual Enlightenment

Make your own affirmation, to stay in balance with the Creative Force within you. You are the Creator of your life and reality. So start using affirmations.

AFFIRMATIONS TO STAY IN BALANCE WITH YOUR CREATIVE FORCE

I can do it.	I am prepared.
I do my best.	I am successful.
I love myself.	I live in the Now (Present).
I am honest.	I am a good student.
I am a good parent.	I understand.
I forgive.	I am at peace.
I live in Truth.	I am Light, and I live in Light.

There are many books on the market about affirmations. Browse and dowse and see if there are some for you to use. Wonderful books of affirmations, written by Louise L. Hay, are *Heart Thoughts, a Treasury of Inner Wisdom* and *Inner Wisdom: Meditations for the Heart and Soul*. I highly recommend them.

I WALK WITH BEAUTY (GOD)

I walk with Beauty (God) before me.

I walk with Beauty (God) behind me.

I walk with Beauty (God) above me.

I walk with Beauty (God) below me.

I walk with Beauty (God) around me.

Native American Prayer

Ask, and it is given; seek, and you find; knock, and it is opened to you.

For every one who asks receives, and he who seeks finds, and to him who knocks it is opened.

St. Matthew 7:7–8

Celebrate life. See yourself as getting lighter and wiser rather than getting older.

Say "Yes" to yourself. Be honest with yourself. Surprise yourself.

EMBRACE THE DIVINE PRINCIPLES OF TRUTH

As you ask, so you receive, my Child.

You know I always give you what your true Soul desires, not what your Will is asking for.

To receive, you also need to embrace and follow the Divine Principles of Truth.

You cannot live an empty life. What does empty mean? Things without spiritual meaning, like materialistic stuff, like more of this and more of that. It does not lead you to Enlightenment; it leads you to distrust, despair and unwillingness to except the Divine Truth within.

I am watching you, my Child.
Embrace me, and you are the THEE of LIGHT.

Amen

CLEAN, CLEARING

What does "clean, clearing" mean?

- Pure, bright, light, radiant, clear within, brilliant, luminous, unclouded, transparent
- To make clean; to free from impurities or removing foreign matter so the cleansed item is without fault
- Clear of darkness within, from confusing thoughts, from discriminating, from distress, from obstruction of energy flow

By letting go negative energies, you allow your Being to get lighter and embrace again the Divine within, pure in thought and deed.

Use your dowsing method to learn whether you need to let go negative energies such as ones listed below:

- Judgement or whatever is unseemly, noxious, offensive, imperfect or defective.
- Guilt, blame, shame, polluted, imprisoned.
- Others. There are more negative energies that you may need to name.

PRAYERS

What does praying mean?

The act of asking for a favor with earnestness, a solemn petition for benefits addressed to the Supreme Being (**to GOD**), the words of a supplication (humble and earnest prayer, request).

Here are a few prayers you may feel in tune with.

&—&—&—&—&—&—&

And when you pray, you shall not be like the hypocrites. For they love to pray standing in the synagogues and on the corners of the streets, that they may be seen by men. Assuredly, I say to you, they have their reward.

But you, when you pray, go into your room, and when you have shut your door, pray to your Father who is in the secret place; and your Father who sees in secret will reward you openly.

And when you pray, do not use vain repetitions as the heathen do. For they think that they will be heard for their many words.

Therefore do not be like them. For your Father knows the things you have need of before you ask him.

St. Matthew 6:5–8

&—&—&—&—&—&—&

After this manner, therefore pray: Our Father in heaven, hallowed be Your name.

Your kingdom come. Your Will be done on Earth as it is in heaven.

Give us this day our daily bread. And forgive us our debts, as we forgive our debtors.

And do not lead us into temptation, but deliver us from the evil one.

For Yours is the kingdom and the power and the glory forever. Amen

"The Lord's Prayer," from St. Matthew 6:9–13
the Authorized (King James) Version of the Bible

I WORK FOR GOD

God's tool I am. What a great honor!

God knows that I can work for him on every earthly corner.

I go wherever I am needed, wherever I am sent.

My heart is open. My mind is clear.

Come, Oh Lord, please take me wherever there is despair.

Amen.

The Lord is my shepherd, I shall not want.

He makes me lie down in green pastures. He leads me beside still waters.

He restores my Soul. He leads me in the paths of righteousness for his name's sake.

Even though I walk through the valley of the shadow of death, I fear no evil: for thou art with me; thy rod and thy staff, they comfort me.

Thou prepares a table before me in the presence of my enemies; thou anoint my head with oil; my cup overflows.

Surely goodness and mercy shall follow me all the days of my life; and I shall dwell in the house of the Lord forever.

Psalm 23

Save me, O God, by thy name, and vindicate me by thy might. Hear my prayer, O God; give ear to the words of my mouth.

Psalm 54:1-2

MEDITATION

What does meditate mean?

To dwell on anything in thought; to cogitate, to ponder, contemplate.

Meditation is like putting a plain bamboo stick in a glass of water and letting it root; the only thing you need to do is "watch" and let the creation of "God" unfold in front of you. It gets rooted and sprouts to a beautiful plant. You are the plant that "God" created, and the only thing you need to do is water yourself every day with positive motivational thoughts and creative energy of the spirit. It is as simple as that.

There are many ways to meditate. Some sit for one half hour in a straight back chair, close their eyes and focus on a mantra. The mantra could be the Twenty-third Psalm, or the Lord's Prayer (listed on the previous page), the word "OHM" or the word "Amen."

If meditating is for you, you may dowse for the kind of meditation that gives you the above highest benefit of growth and relaxation. Meditate where and on what you feel comfortable. Whatever is right for you, works for you; accept it as your Divine Truth. There are many books available on meditation; search for the one which feels right for you.

&—&—&—&—&—&—&

A MESSAGE TO ANNELIESE: "I CREATE AND I ALSO TAKE"

In 1991, I received a message from "God" telling me "*I CREATE AND I ALSO TAKE.*" I knew in my mind that someone was going to die. I did not know at that time it was my father. I thought it was my husband's cousin in France, who was battling bladder cancer at that time; he is still alive (he received a new bladder made from his large intestine).

A month later, I had a vision in which I saw my Dad in his blue suit (and that is what we buried him in). Then I knew my father was going to die. After that I received many poems about heaven, golden gates, lots of light, etc. I sent these poems to my father (Vater), and he asked me, "What do you have with God and all this things?"

I was not in tune with God before that incident. In Germany, as children we had only a little religious upbringing. We attended church only for Christmas, so our parents could set up the Christmas tree, and when we came home the Weihnachtsman (Saint Nicholas) was there, a tradition at that time in their lives. When we were 14 years old, we had to go for two years to Confirmation class once a week to be confirmed. And, as adults in the United States, we sent our two daughters to a Lutheran parochial school, because we felt we could not give them religion.

When I found out the diagnosis, pancreatic cancer, from the test they did in the hospital on my father, that my father had only five months to live, I kept a journal, by writing to "God" every day. I felt it helped keep me sane. I talked to God, and he gave me answers.

&—&—&—&—&—&—&

I still do this today, not every day. I ask God if he has a message for me, and if my head shakes yes, I write it down. I never know what I've received until I read it later. In general, I do this with a cup of coffee on the kitchen table. Here is an example of what I do; this came by asking when I was writing this book, *Search for My Spiritual Enlightenment.*

Dear Lord, thank you for all the beautiful gifts you give me every day.

For the flowers which bloom in front of me, for the sun and moon which are shining on us, for the people I meet every day, for my family physically and spiritually, my husband of 43 years, for my children, and my grandchildren which are actually yours. I give thanks for the food you put in front of me, for the bed I sleep in, for nature and mankind, for being able to share with others your vibration of Unconditional Love.

I thank you for everything. I am now ready to receive your message.

• • •

My Beautiful Child, you are a supreme, beautiful being.

You are always ready to help others in need, often with a blessed gesture from me. You do know I work through you, for you committed to me to be my disciple of Truth. You promised to share yourself with others and help them find me. As you know, the me is you and is everyone who sees themselves as Divine Beings of Love and Light.

I know you always tell them, "The Divine is within you, give up your free Will and embrace my Will, the Divinity within yourself." You did it, my Child, and you know it was simple.

You know, with giving up your free Will, you are responsible for sharing me with others, telling others about the Purpose of life, Learning, Growth within the Divine Principles of Truth. And you know you wrote about them in this book of Spiritual Enlightenment. You are always in tune with me, and it is so exciting to talk with you in your journal of Enlightenment. By giving up earthly things, you receive so much more than you ever thought you could receive from me.

I am totally the energy of Divine Truth, just like you are my Child, for we are One forever. Amen.

• • •

Thank you dear Lord for your message.
Forever yours, your Anneliese. February 2, 2001.

Using the Inner Art of Dowsing in the Search for My Spiritual Enlightenment

I also receive from "God" lots of beautiful poetry, which lifts my spirit.

So this is something you may like to do also, as a method of meditation. It works for me. I also feel I was ready to accept the Supreme Being (Source) within me at that time, and from then on forward, my life totally changed.

I am not a Christian; I am a Disciple of God, the Highest Source of existence for me. We all may have a different pronunciation for the Highest Source and it is OK. Accept the one with whom you have the highest connection.

CREATIVE VISUALIZATION

What does creative visualization mean?

- Visual, pertaining to sight, used in sight; serving as the instrument of seeing, the angle formed at the eye by the rays of light from the extremities of the object
- Using the Art of Mental Energy and Affirmation
- Using our mental energy for transforming ourselves into the energies of health, wealth, happiness and harmony, into beings of Love, Light and Divinity

It is important to relax and let the vibration of God's desire come into you.

There are many books on the book market that you may like to investigate. Again, search out one that is for above your Highest Good of spiritual growth.

SACRED OBJECTS: SYMBOLS, DREAMS, TALISMANS AND JEWELRY

There are many sacred objects you may relate to. Dowse or tune in to your Inner Knowing to find one that is right for you, then stay in tune with it. You may in the future use a different one; it all depends on your spiritual growth. Remember, you are in charge; no one but you, only you, can push you to the finish line. You can surrender to God, and let him guide you where he feels you need to travel. Again it is simple; trusting is the Key.

Symbol. An object animate or inanimate to call up something moral or intellectual; an emblem; a type of sign (the olive branch is the symbol of peace); a distinctive mark; a creed or confession of Faith; nature symbols, words, investing of objects or animals with symbolic meaning (from *Webster's Encyclopedic Dictionary*).

Dreams as symbols. Awakening to our Inner Knowing can give us guidance for daily living. A dream is an image, thought, or emotion that occurs during sleep. There are many books on the market that can explain and help you understand meanings of dreams.

Talismans. A talisman is a magical figure, which if you believe, may preserve the bearer from injury, disease, evils, or sudden death; it is something that produces extraordinary effects. Often a symbol, charm, or amulet is good to use as a talisman. If you believe that they may help you on your journey of Enlightenment, please use them.

Jewelry. I like to wear jewelry; it makes me feel dressed. I especially love jewelry from India and Native American jewelry; it gives me a feeling of connectedness, of being in tune with the bearers of Truth. We have forgotten the true meaning of Nature, of GOD in the form of Nature. We need to remember <u>we came from dust and return to dust</u> (our Shell external).

ONENESS WITHIN: MESSAGES TO PONDER

These are messages (sayings, thoughts, ideas, and quotes) that may help you on your search for Spiritual Enlightenment.

FLOWER OF ENLIGHTENMENT

I am looking at a flower.

It came from a seed of a flower, which was blown by the wind to a speck of dirt (earth).

There it settled. And when the rain came, it got watered, and it sprouted into a green blade.

From there it grew; we still did not know what it would look like. It grew taller and taller until it reached the right length, so it could look out to the world to the eyes of the seer. It opened slowly for it needed nourishment of sun, water, air and elements of Earth.

As it opened to its full color, it also needed time to develop in its right size, right essence, and right energy of the Soul.

That is what you are. You are a seed that grows into this beautiful flower of Enlightenment. Until you accept yourself, can you be accepted by others?

Again, stay in balance before the Throne of God.

TO EMBRACE THE DIVINE

You are the Pillow I can dream on.
You are the Pillar I can lean on.
You are the Place I can pray to.
You are the Peace I can receive.
You are the Power I can embrace.
You are the everlasting Truth I can live in.
You are the Divine for me, the Temple of Hope.

You are my God.

Thank you. Amen

DEAR EGO, LET GO

We may ask our Ego to let go of materialistic view points, to come into the sacred space of Truth, and work with the Divine Vibration within us.

Attitudes and words are the Keys to Enlightenment.

Wrong thinking gets you back into the past.

&—&—&—&—&—&—&

My mouth shall speak the praise of the Lord: and let all flesh bless his holy name for ever and ever.

Psalm 145:21

&—&—&—&—&—&—&

FOR EVERY END THERE IS A NEW BEGINNING

For every end there is a new beginning, a new way of life.

We leave behind some sorrows, hurt and pain. And in the new beginning we gain new understanding, new thoughts and new feelings, seeing new horizons, meeting new opportunities, experiencing Unconditional Love— for we give it out, and we receive the love we came to feel.

I am ready to leave yesterday, ready to enjoy and experience every moment in the moment and let the sun rise tomorrow as a new day, a New Beginning.

Anneliese Hagemann

&—&—&—&—&—&—&

TIME TO MOVE ON

It is time for me to move on.

It is time to see the stars, the moon and the sun.

It is time to explore the unknown.

It is time to experience a new way of living, loving and caring.

It is time to live in God's Truth, God's Unconditional Love, and God's Way.

It is time, and the time is now.

Anneliese Hagemann

Using the Inner Art of Dowsing in the Search for My Spiritual Enlightenment

Something to think about: we are the Computer.

Everything else is just a printout.
What you need you keep, what you don't need, you delete.

EVERYTHING is ENERGY.

Every word you think, speak, and write creates a reaction within and
around your world.
Be creative in a positive way.

Today is the day to explore the unknown.

The unknown in your mind is the knowing in your Soul.

Your own Will comes to pass.

The Divine Will within you shines in your Heart and Soul.

Our Soul is the Core of life.

It can not exist apart on planet Earth by itself.
The Soul is beyond form and words.

INNER LIGHT

The Lord giveth Light, and we reign in it forever.

Let your Inner Light shine with God's Golden Light and Truth.

Let your sunshine stay in Truth with the Divine.

I am Light at all times, the simplicity of Enlightenment.

Lighthearted with the flow is the only way to go
on our way of Enlightenment.

☗—☗—☗—☗—☗—☗—☗

DELIGHTFUL GIFTS ABOUND

Delightful Music, delightful Soul,

Delightful Embracement with God's Soul,

Delightful Colors, delightful Stones, all of these give us
energy to nourish our Souls.

What beautiful gifts we have around us, if we only have our eyes and ears
open to receive the message from above.

My children, are you hearing me? Are you getting my message?

I embrace your Heart and Soul, your Total Being, You/Me.

☗—☗—☗—☗—☗—☗—☗

FREEDOM IS OUR BATTLE CRY

Freedom is our battle cry, Freedom from pain, anger and hurt, etc.

Freedom to explore the unknown, to enjoy life to the fullest,

Freedom from physical commitment, Freedom to speak our Truth.

Freedom means Truth. Amen

Doris and Anneliese Hagemann

☗—☗—☗—☗—☗—☗—☗

As I am so are you, Pure Divine Truth, as I am so are you.

☗—☗—☗—☗—☗—☗—☗

DO I EXPRESS OR SUPPRESS THE TRUTH?

Admiration—to express the Truth.

Suppress—we suppress the Truth about "Onement."

☗—☗—☗—☗—☗—☗—☗

I Am the Light: receive it.

I Am Unconditional Love: accept it.
I Am Peace: acknowledge it.
I Am Truth: know it.
I Am You: the Light forever.

Amen

Using the Inner Art of Dowsing in the Search for My Spiritual Enlightenment

BEAUTY IS FREE

The Beauty from you, dear Lord, is free,
The mountain, the land, the sky and the sea,
To roam, to feel, to taste, to smell, to touch and to see.

Come on, you humans, wake up, walk and use your key!

Your key is your heart, the Center of Thee,
The treasure our Lord has provided for you and me.

Pray, meditate, believe, and you are free
To explore and experience
The Beauty from and within Thee.

Amen

COME INTO THE LIGHT

Come out from the darkness of the night, where you
have been hiding your Soul.
Come into the Light where Love, Truth and Life reside.
You experience lightening of your heavy load.
You receive guidance from above with Love.

So, my child, instead of the dark night, see my heavenly Light.

Amen

DISSOLVING AN OBSTACLE

Go out of the ship.
Get around it or drown with it.
Work with it.

&—&—&—&—&—&—&

POSITIVE F, FREE FOREVER FORMULA

To have Freedom means to "move Forward" by
Forgiving, Forgetting, and being Fulfilled.

Also, you need to Feel Fortunate and to be Filled with Faith.

Build a strong Foundation for the Future without Fear or Friction.

Allow yourself to Feel the Freedom of your Soul in Flight.

Doris and Anneliese Hagemann

&—&—&—&—&—&—&

COME, JOIN ME

You are awake, you are with me,

Your thoughts are mine of Purity.

I love you, my Infinite Purity Souls.

Come on, walk with, through Eternity.

Hallelujah, Hallelujah, Hallelujah.

&—&—&—&—&—&—&

GRADUATION POEM

It is now time for Graduation, a time to move on.

With trust guiding us to new places, our protection of God's Light we don.

We fly over mountain, deserts, and valleys,
across oceans, rivers, and streams.

Swim as dolphins in underwater cities remembering
from long time ago in our dreams.

Feel the sky as we soar as eagles using our treasured gifts of sight.

We are here to share an important message as Angels of
peace, truth and Light.

The message is our "Inner Knowing" deep within all the time.

It is now time for all to remember we are truly "Most Divine."

Geraldine Kozlowski and Anneliese Gabriel Hagemann

BIBLIOGRAPHY

CITATIONS IN THIS BOOK

- Amber, Reuben. ©1991. *Color Therapy*. Aurora Press, Inc. ISBN: 0943358043.

- Andrews, Ted. ©1993. *Animal-Speak, The Spiritual and Magical Powers of Creatures Great and Small*. Llewellyn Publications. ISBN: 0875420281.

- Bible verses are from the Authorized (King James) Version of the Bible.

- Bowers, Barbara, Ph.D. ©1989. *What Color Is Your Aura?* Pocket Books. ISBN: 0671707639.

- Bull, John and Farrand, John, Jr. ©1977. *The Audubon Society: Field Guide to North American Birds, Eastern Region*. Alfred A. Knopf, Inc. ISBN: 0394414051.

- Coombes, Allen J. ©1992. *DK Handbooks: Trees*. Dorling Kindersley, Inc. ISBN: 156458075X.

- Dolfyn. ©1993. *Angels* chart. Earthspirit, Inc.

- Dan Dupuis, Richard Krull. ©1992. *Creating Your Light Body*. Onion Publishing Co. ISBN: 0963134183.

- Einstein, Albert (quote). *The American Dowser, Quarterly Digest*. 37 (Spring 1997). The American Society of Dowsers, Inc. See *Note 1*.

- Foster, Steven and Duke, James A. ©1990. *Peterson Field Guide Series: A Field Guide to Medicinal Plants, Eastern and Central North America*. Houghton Mifflin Company. ISBN: 0395467225.

- Gerber, Richard, M.D. ©c2000. *A Practical Guide to Vibrational Medicine*. Quill, an imprint of Harper Collins. ISBN: 0060959371.

- Hagemann, Anneliese Gabriel. See *Books from 3 H Dowsing International*, below.

- Hay, Louise L. ©1990. *Heart Thoughts: A Treasury of Inner Wisdom*. Hay House, Inc. ISBN: 1561700002.

- Hay, Louise L. ©2000. *Inner Wisdom: Meditations for the Heart and Soul*. Hay House, Inc. ISBN: 1561707295.

- Hopman, Ellen Evert. ©1992. *Tree Medicine, Tree Magic*. Phoenix Publications, Inc.

- Kloss, Jethro. ©1995. *Back to Eden*. Revised and expanded second edition. Back to Eden Books Publishing Co. ISBN: 0940985101.

- Kroeger, Rev. Hanna. ©1995. *Spices to the Rescue*. Hanna Kroeger Publications. See *Note 2*.

- Lust, John. ©1974. *The Herb Book*. Bantam Books. ISBN: 0553267701.

- Melody. ©1991. *Love is in the Earth, a Kaleidoscope of Crystals*. Earth-Love Publishing House. ISBN: 096281900x

- Melody. ©1993, *Love is in the Earth, Mineralogical Pictorial*. Earth-Love Publishing House. ISBN: 0962819026

- Rain, Mary Summer. ©1990 *Earthway*. Pocket Books. ISBN: 0671706675.

(continued on the next page)

(continued from the previous page)

- Thie, John F., D.C. ©1994. *Touch for Health*. Revised edition. DeVorss Publications. ISBN: 0875161804. See *Note 3*.

- Udvardy, Miklos. D. F. ©1977. *The Audubon Society: Field Guide to North American Birds, Western Region*. Alfred A. Knopf, Inc. ISBN: 0394414101.

- Venning, Frank D. and Manabu, Saito C. ©1984. *Wild Flowers of North America: A Guide to Field Identification*. Golden Press; Western Pub. Co. ISBN: 0307136647 (pbk).

- Wauters, Ambika. ©1997. *Chakras and Their Archetypes*. The Crossing Press. ISBN: 0895948915 (pbk).

- Wauters, Ambika. ©1998. *Healing with the Energy of the Chakras*. The Crossing Press. ISBN: 0895949067.

- Whitaker, John O. ©1980. *The Audubon Society: Field Guide to North American Mammals*. Alfred A. Knopf, Inc. ISBN: 0394507622.

- Yarbro, Chelsea Quinn. ©1979. *Messages from Michael*. Berkly Books. ISBN: 0425104370.

Note 1. The American Society of Dowsers (ASD) can be contacted at PO Box 24, Danville, VT 05828. Web site address is http://www.dowsers.org. The ASD Bookstore phone number is 1-800-711-9497.

Note 2. For information about this book, contact Hanna's Herb Shop, 5684 Valmont Road, Boulder, CO 80301, 1-800-206-6722, 1-303-443-0755, www.hannasherbshop.com.

Note 3. For information about this book, contact Touch for Health Kinesiology Association, 1-800-466-8342, http://www.tfhka.org.

BOOKS FROM 3 H DOWSING INTERNATIONAL

- Hagemann, Anneliese Gabriel. ©2000. *Dowsing/Divining*. Revised edition. 3 H Dowsing International. ISBN: 0965665313.
  This booklet is an introduction to Dowsing/Divining, a wonderful way of ancient Knowledge, to be used in finding and tapping into our Inner Knowing, Inner Truth. It describes dowsing and how we can apply it in our daily life. It includes charts and diagrams.

- Hagemann, Anneliese Gabriel. ©2000. *A Quick Gauge to Body, Mind, Spirit Wellness Immune System Balancer*. 3 H Dowsing International. ISBN: 096566533X.
  This booklet teaches how to apply dowsing to keep your Immune System balanced on a daily basis. It includes charts.

- Hagemann, Anneliese Gabriel and Hagemann, Doris Katherine. ©1999. Revised edition. *To Our Health. Using the Inner Art of Dowsing in the Search for Health-Happiness-Harmony in Body-Mind-Spirit*.
  3 H Dowsing International. ISBN: 0965665305.
  This is our first workbook in its third edition, created after illnesses and feeling out of tune for many

lifetimes. It guides us through a 13-step method of self-healing and self-empowerment. It goes right down to the Core issues we are harboring within. With this book, we can clear all channels of existence.

- Hagemann, Anneliese Gabriel. ©2000. *Using the Inner Art of Dowsing in the Search for My Life's Path—Soul Mission*. 3 H Dowsing International. ISBN: 0965665313.
  This book guides us through a nine-step method. We learn who we truly are, what unfinished business we need to take care of, including fears, patterns, habits, etc. that are holding us back from Spiritual Enlightenment.

How to obtain the books

Books listed above are used in the Inner Art of Dowsing classes taught worldwide by 3 H Dowsing International facilitators.

Books are also available from the following sources:

- 3 H Dowsing International
  Anneliese Gabriel Hagemann
  W10160, County Road C
  Wautoma, WI 54982 U.S.A.
  1-920-787-4747
  ilovedowsing@hotmail.com

- New Leaf Distribution, Wholesaler
  1-800-326-2665

- American Society of Dowsers
  1-800-711-9497
  http://www.dowsers.org

- On the web at http://www.get-intuit.com

- On the web at http://www.Amazon.com

INDEX

&—&—&—&—&—&—&—&

DELIGHTFUL GIFTS ABOUND

Delightful Music, delightful Soul,

Delightful Embracement with God's Soul,

Delightful Colors, delightful Stones, all of these give us
energy to nourish our Souls.

What beautiful gifts we have around us, if we only have our eyes and ears
open to receive the message from above.

My children, are you hearing me? Are you getting my message?

I embrace your Heart and Soul, your Total Being, You/Me.

&—&—&—&—&—&—&—&

FREEDOM IS OUR BATTLE CRY

Freedom is our battle cry, Freedom from pain, anger and hurt, etc.

Freedom to explore the unknown, to enjoy life to the fullest,

Freedom from physical commitment, Freedom to speak our Truth.

Freedom means Truth. Amen
Doris and Anneliese Hagemann

&—&—&—&—&—&—&—&

As I am so are you, Pure Divine Truth, as I am so are you.

&—&—&—&—&—&—&—&

DO I EXPRESS OR SUPPRESS THE TRUTH?

Admiration—to express the Truth.

Suppress—we suppress the Truth about "Onement."

&—&—&—&—&—&—&—&

I Am the Light: receive it.

I Am Unconditional Love: accept it.
I Am Peace: acknowledge it.
I Am Truth: know it.
I Am You: the Light forever.

Amen

Using the Inner Art of Dowsing in the Search for My Spiritual Enlightenment

BEAUTY IS FREE

The Beauty from you, dear Lord, is free,
The mountain, the land, the sky and the sea,
To roam, to feel, to taste, to smell, to touch and to see.

Come on, you humans, wake up, walk and use your key!

Your key is your heart, the Center of Thee,
The treasure our Lord has provided for you and me.

Pray, meditate, believe, and you are free
To explore and experience
The Beauty from and within Thee.

Amen

COME INTO THE LIGHT

Come out from the darkness of the night, where you
have been hiding your Soul.
Come into the Light where Love, Truth and Life reside.
You experience lightening of your heavy load.
You receive guidance from above with Love.

So, my child, instead of the dark night, see my heavenly Light.

Amen

DISSOLVING AN OBSTACLE

Go out of the ship.
Get around it or drown with it.
Work with it.

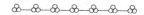

POSITIVE F, FREE FOREVER FORMULA

To have Freedom means to "move Forward" by
Forgiving, Forgetting, and being Fulfilled.

Also, you need to Feel Fortunate and to be Filled with Faith.

Build a strong Foundation for the Future without Fear or Friction.

Allow yourself to Feel the Freedom of your Soul in Flight.

Doris and Anneliese Hagemann

COME, JOIN ME

You are awake, you are with me,

Your thoughts are mine of Purity.

I love you, my Infinite Purity Souls.

Come on, walk with, through Eternity.

Hallelujah, Hallelujah, Hallelujah.

GRADUATION POEM

It is now time for Graduation, a time to move on.

With trust guiding us to new places, our protection of God's Light we don.

We fly over mountain, deserts, and valleys,
across oceans, rivers, and streams.

Swim as dolphins in underwater cities remembering
from long time ago in our dreams.

Feel the sky as we soar as eagles using our treasured gifts of sight.

We are here to share an important message as Angels of
peace, truth and Light.

The message is our "Inner Knowing" deep within all the time.

It is now time for all to remember we are truly "Most Divine."

Geraldine Kozlowski and Anneliese Gabriel Hagemann

BIBLIOGRAPHY

CITATIONS IN THIS BOOK

- Amber, Reuben. ©1991. *Color Therapy*. Aurora Press, Inc. ISBN: 0943358043.

- Andrews, Ted. ©1993. *Animal-Speak, The Spiritual and Magical Powers of Creatures Great and Small*. Llewellyn Publications. ISBN: 0875420281.

- Bible verses are from the Authorized (King James) Version of the Bible.

- Bowers, Barbara, Ph.D. ©1989. *What Color Is Your Aura?* Pocket Books. ISBN: 0671707639.

- Bull, John and Farrand, John, Jr. ©1977. *The Audubon Society: Field Guide to North American Birds, Eastern Region*. Alfred A. Knopf, Inc. ISBN: 0394414051.

- Coombes, Allen J. ©1992. *DK Handbooks: Trees*. Dorling Kindersley, Inc. ISBN: 156458075X.

- Dolfyn. ©1993. *Angels* chart. Earthspirit, Inc.

- Dan Dupuis, Richard Krull. ©1992. *Creating Your Light Body*. Onion Publishing Co. ISBN: 0963134183.

- Einstein, Albert (quote). *The American Dowser, Quarterly Digest*. 37 (Spring 1997). The American Society of Dowsers, Inc. See *Note 1*.

- Foster, Steven and Duke, James A. ©1990. *Peterson Field Guide Series: A Field Guide to Medicinal Plants, Eastern and Central North America*. Houghton Mifflin Company. ISBN: 0395467225.

- Gerber, Richard, M.D. ©c2000. *A Practical Guide to Vibrational Medicine*. Quill, an imprint of Harper Collins. ISBN: 0060959371.

- Hagemann, Anneliese Gabriel. See *Books from 3 H Dowsing International*, below.

- Hay, Louise L. ©1990. *Heart Thoughts: A Treasury of Inner Wisdom*. Hay House, Inc. ISBN: 1561700002.

- Hay, Louise L. ©2000. *Inner Wisdom: Meditations for the Heart and Soul*. Hay House, Inc. ISBN: 1561707295.

- Hopman, Ellen Evert. ©1992. *Tree Medicine, Tree Magic*. Phoenix Publications, Inc.

- Kloss, Jethro. ©1995. *Back to Eden*. Revised and expanded second edition. Back to Eden Books Publishing Co. ISBN: 0940985101.

- Kroeger, Rev. Hanna. ©1995. *Spices to the Rescue*. Hanna Kroeger Publications. See *Note 2*.

- Lust, John. ©1974. *The Herb Book*. Bantam Books. ISBN: 0553267701.

- Melody. ©1991. *Love is in the Earth, a Kaleidoscope of Crystals*. Earth-Love Publishing House. ISBN: 096281900x

- Melody. ©1993, *Love is in the Earth, Mineralogical Pictorial*. Earth-Love Publishing House. ISBN: 0962819026

- Rain, Mary Summer. ©1990 *Earthway*. Pocket Books. ISBN: 0671706675.

(continued on the next page)

(continued from the previous page)

- Thie, John F., D.C. ©1994. *Touch for Health.* Revised edition. DeVorss Publications. ISBN: 0875161804. See *Note 3.*

- Udvardy, Miklos. D. F. ©1977. *The Audubon Society: Field Guide to North American Birds, Western Region.* Alfred A. Knopf, Inc. ISBN: 0394414101.

- Venning, Frank D. and Manabu, Saito C. ©1984. *Wild Flowers of North America: A Guide to Field Identification.* Golden Press; Western Pub. Co. ISBN: 0307136647 (pbk).

- Wauters, Ambika. ©1997. *Chakras and Their Archetypes.* The Crossing Press. ISBN: 0895948915 (pbk).

- Wauters, Ambika. ©1998. *Healing with the Energy of the Chakras.* The Crossing Press. ISBN: 0895949067.

- Whitaker, John O. ©1980. *The Audubon Society: Field Guide to North American Mammals.* Alfred A. Knopf, Inc. ISBN: 0394507622.

- Yarbro, Chelsea Quinn. ©1979. *Messages from Michael.* Berkly Books. ISBN: 0425104370.

Note 1. The American Society of Dowsers (ASD) can be contacted at PO Box 24, Danville, VT 05828. Web site address is http://www.dowsers.org. The ASD Bookstore phone number is 1-800-711-9497.

Note 2. For information about this book, contact Hanna's Herb Shop, 5684 Valmont Road, Boulder, CO 80301, 1-800-206-6722, 1-303-443-0755, www.hannasherbshop.com.

Note 3. For information about this book, contact Touch for Health Kinesiology Association, 1-800-466-8342, http://www.tfhka.org.

BOOKS FROM 3 H DOWSING INTERNATIONAL

- Hagemann, Anneliese Gabriel. ©2000. *Dowsing/Divining.* Revised edition. 3 H Dowsing International. ISBN: 0965665313.
  This booklet is an introduction to Dowsing/Divining, a wonderful way of ancient Knowledge, to be used in finding and tapping into our Inner Knowing, Inner Truth. It describes dowsing and how we can apply it in our daily life. It includes charts and diagrams.

- Hagemann, Anneliese Gabriel. ©2000. *A Quick Gauge to Body, Mind, Spirit Wellness Immune System Balancer.* 3 H Dowsing International. ISBN: 096566533X.
  This booklet teaches how to apply dowsing to keep your Immune System balanced on a daily basis. It includes charts.

- Hagemann, Anneliese Gabriel and Hagemann, Doris Katherine. ©1999. Revised edition. *To Our Health. Using the Inner Art of Dowsing in the Search for Health-Happiness-Harmony in Body-Mind-Spirit.*
  3 H Dowsing International. ISBN: 0965665305.
  This is our first workbook in its third edition, created after illnesses and feeling out of tune for many

lifetimes. It guides us through a 13-step method of self-healing and self-empowerment. It goes right down to the Core issues we are harboring within. With this book, we can clear all channels of existence.

- Hagemann, Anneliese Gabriel. ©2000. *Using the Inner Art of Dowsing in the Search for My Life's Path–Soul Mission*. 3 H Dowsing International. ISBN: 0965665313.
This book guides us through a nine-step method. We learn who we truly are, what unfinished business we need to take care of, including fears, patterns, habits, etc. that are holding us back from Spiritual Enlightenment.

How to obtain the books

Books listed above are used in the Inner Art of Dowsing classes taught worldwide by 3 H Dowsing International facilitators.

Books are also available from the following sources:

- 3 H Dowsing International
  Anneliese Gabriel Hagemann
  W10160, County Road C
  Wautoma, WI 54982 U.S.A.
  1-920-787-4747
  ilovedowsing@hotmail.com

- New Leaf Distribution, Wholesaler
  1-800-326-2665

- American Society of Dowsers
  1-800-711-9497
  http://www.dowsers.org

- On the web at http://www.get-intuit.com

- On the web at http://www.Amazon.com

INDEX